The Art of Anastasia

A TWENTIETH CENTURY FOX PRESENTATION

The Art of
ANASTASIA™

TEXT BY

HARVEY DENEROFF

INTRODUCTIONS BY

DON BLUTH AND GARY GOLDMAN

HarperCollins*Publishers*

Design and art direction by Michael James Walsh

FIRST EDITION

ISBN 0-06-757530-7

97 98 99 00 01/10 9 8 7 6 5 4 3 2 1

PRINTED AND BOUND BY WORZALLA PUBLISHING CO.

STEVENS POINT, WISCONSIN

HARPERCOLLINS STAFF:

Creative Director: Joseph Montebello
Editor: Beth Bortz
Production Editor: Christine Tanigawa
Production Manager: Dianne Walber

"Anastasia self-portrait" on page 1 is reproduced
from the book The Romanovs, Love, power & tragedy
ISBN 0-9521644-0X by permission of Leppi Publication-London.

Photos on page 32 are
reproduced from the book Tsar
ISBN 0-316-50787-3 by permission of Peter Kurth.

Art credits appear on page 192.

CONTENTS

Author's Note 6
Introduction by Don Bluth 8
Introduction by Gary Goldman 10

I.
The Past Is Prologue 13
The Romanovs
Anastasia: Myth and Reality
Anna Anderson on Stage, Screen, and Television
The Prologue

II.
Journey to St. Petersburg 46
A Matter of Style
Characters: Anya
Characters: Pooka
Anatomy of a Frame: Bartok and the Reliquary
Creating Multitudes of Characters
The Catherine Palace Ballroom

III.
By Land and Sea 87
Characters: Rasputin and Bartok
Animation Meets Technology: The Train Wreck
Characters: Dimitri and Vladimir
Nightmare at Sea

IV.
Paris 123
Paris in the 1920s
Paris Holds the Key to Your Heart
History Meets Fantasy: Marie's Bedroom
Characters: Marie and Sophie
Music and Song

V.
Coda 177
Fabergé Eggs
Happily Ever After

Acknowledgments and Credits 192

Author's Note

In writing *The Art of Anastasia*, I have concentrated on the film and the artists who made it. However, in order to truly understand the significance of *Anastasia*, it is also important to recognize Twentieth Century Fox's decision to get involved with animated features and the collaborative effort that went into this development. ➤ William Mechanic, chairman and CEO of Fox Filmed Entertainment, is one of a new breed of movie executives who have come to realize that animation can be made as much for adults as for children. He and others like him are making possible the long-held dream of American animators to take animation from the fringes into the mainstream of the film and television industry. ➤ Mechanic came to Fox from Disney, where he headed up several divisions. He had initially been reluctant to take the job at Disney: "I was uninterested in all the current Disney animated films and didn't find the form appealing anymore. I thought that the best work had been done in the past and the films in the seventies and eighties had become stultified. But during my stay there, I really learned to love animated films again, and by the time I left, I liked them better than other pictures." ➤ In 1993, while negotiating for his current position at Fox with Rupert Murdoch, "I read a small item in *Variety* that the Bluth Studios in Ireland had been acquired by Murdoch as part of his takeover of Star TV in Hong Kong. I showed it to Rupert and said, 'I don't know if I can take this job or not, but if I do, this is really important to me. Even if I don't, I think you should pay attention to Bluth. You actually have a resource of major proportions in Don, and you ought to focus on it. But if you really want me here, make sure this is intact.' At that time, the studio [which was experiencing financial problems] was falling apart. By the time I took the job, the company had collapsed, but it was the first thing I jumped on." ➤ He adds, "I've always appreciated Bluth's and Goldman's movies, especially during my nine years at Disney. The quality of their work is great, and when they were working with a decent script, they made a good movie. [The problem was] they were better than their material. And my deal with Don and Gary was, we'd work on the material together. I felt that if we could put our storytelling together with their animation skills, and put the marketing resources of a major company behind them, we could really be ambitious. To me, it's no fun if you're not ambitious." ➤ The result was Fox Animation Studios, in Phoenix, which was initially staffed with artists who had worked with Don Bluth and Gary Goldman in Dublin. In addition, Mechanic hired Christopher Meledandri to head Fox Family Films. He did not have the same sort of animation background, as Meledandri notes he "had been working, inadvertently, on movies, like *Cool Runnings*, that turned out to be ones that families went to see. ➤ "This coincided with the birth of my son," Meledandri adds. "So, the idea of making movies that could be shared by different generations was something that appealed to me, both as a movie-goer and as somebody who was involved in storytelling. Animation was something that I discovered through the eyes of my son." ⬳ Meledandri teamed with two experienced animation hands from Disney, Kevin Bannerman as vice president of production, Fox Family Films, and Maureen Donley as executive producer. ⬳ While this sort of commitment might seem obvious in any studio involved in animated films, this has not always been the case. It really wasn't until the resurgence of animation at Disney under Michael Eisner, Jeffrey Katzenberg, and Roy Disney, along with the early success of such Bluth films as *An American Tail* and *The Land Before Time*, that animation began to be taken seriously. ⬳ Bill Mechanic explains that, in making *Anastasia*, "I was very keen not to make a kids' picture. Everybody kept trying to write it for children, as they want to do with all these movies, and insult the intelligence of the children and (even more so) the adults. I hated sitting through those movies with my daughter and was really focused on us avoiding that." ⬳ This focus was helped by the way in which artists and executives worked together. As Chris Meledandri points out, "The development of *Anastasia* was a collaborative process. Somebody might look at that process and say, 'There's no way you can have that many people involved and not end up reducing the story to the lowest common denominator.' I feel the key to having a large group be a benefit to the process, rather than a liability, is that, at the beginning, you all have to agree on what is the essence of the movie. And if you all join forces to set out to reach that goal with your storytelling, then all of the voices work in service of reaching that goal." ⬳ But what was the "essence" of this particular version of *Anastasia*? The answer to that question revealed itself only after the producers, directors, songwriters, and screenwriters locked themselves into a hotel con-

ference room with a bulletin board and some 3 x 5 index cards. Maureen Donley explains, "We worked until we had an outline that made us happy and then pitched that to the studio. After incorporating their feedback, we finally had in our hands a blueprint for the movie. Now our task was to put some meat on those bones and bring it all to life. Writers Susan Gauthier and Bruce Graham went off to generate a first draft, composer Lynn Ahrens and lyricist Stephen Flaherty immediately went to work on the remaining song score, and since we knew 'Once Upon a December' would be part of our story no matter what, that song was the first piece of the movie to go into storyboarding and then production." ⬳ That meant that there were quite a few plates to keep spinning at the same time. The challenge was to keep identifying sequences of the movie that could go into production while buying time for others to grow into their full potential. The producers had to figure out a way to feed the production monster without sacrificing any story quality. ⬳ However, in the end, the final responsibility for the film rests in the hands of Bluth, Goldman, and the hundreds of artists who worked under them. Bluth and Goldman have been working on their own films together since they left Disney in 1979 and seem to have an intimate knowledge of what the other is doing and thinking. "When we start a film," Goldman says, "we're both involved in preproduction, attending story and writing meetings. Don usually leads with character design, layout, art direction, and storyboard. We work together with the animators in character animation. Once we agree that it's going in the right direction, then I usually take on the line production details, special effects, and pushing for as much production value as possible. Don keeps feeding the production from preproduction." It is this process and the artistic decisions that went into creating *Anastasia* that form much of the backbone of this book. ⬳

Introduction by Don Bluth

Maybe you've heard the story of the scorpion who asked the frog if he would be so kind as to ferry him across a great river. "Right," laughed the frog. "You'll sting me; I'll die and you'll drown." "I promise I won't," pleaded the little scorpion. His face had an expression of such sincerity that it softened the heart of the frog. So the frog steadied himself as the scorpion climbed upon his back, then he swam out into the river. Suddenly he felt a sting on the back of his neck. "Monster!" screamed the wounded frog. "Now we must both perish—how could you do that?" Tears filled the eyes of the little scorpion. "I couldn't help myself," he wept. "It is just in my nature." Poor little scorpion. I understand his unexplained behavior: I too have a nature most compelling. I like to draw. I can trace this magnificent obsession back as far as age three, and beyond that, there are even family photos of me as a baby sucking pencil erasers—no breasts, no bottles—only erasers. As I worked my way through childhood and puberty, this curious, divine calling grew. It became a hungry giant who demanded pencil-to-paper sessions with such ferocity that other areas of my personal development sagged. The big artistic guy inside me whom I named "Oscar" had also discovered animation, and that's when he decided we were going to work for Walt. I was milking the cows with my dad and my older brother one day when these words tumbled off my tongue: "I'm going to be an animator, Dad, and work for Walt Disney." There was silence; the loud squirts of milk in the buckets stopped. "A what?" asked Dad. "An animator." I returned. "Was this the reason I was born?" I asked myself. "To become an animator—or was it just Oscar pushing me around again? He was so ambitious and liked to monopolize my time and thoughts. I had the fingers to hold a pencil and he needed that to express himself. Together, in 1955, we finally began our career at Disney. It was great! While animating there in 1972 I met someone who turned out to be a plot point in my life's story—Gary Goldman. We shared the common desire to restore and lift the art of animation to new heights. Oscar took to him immediately. There were many passionate discussions about "toon art" among the young artists, but no one dared label the emptiness we all felt. Box office receipts were dropping, so something had to be done. My birthday is September 13. That is the day Gary, myself, and fifteen others left Disney to embark on the great adventure we called "Make Animation Better." This odyssey brought serendipity at every turn. It took us to Europe to discover new cultures, new music, new legends and heroes, and a brilliant staff of artists. I eventually became aware of the labyrinth through which an animation film producer must pass to finish a movie. It is a maze with a dimly lit path, booby-trapped with political intrigue, overinflated egos, and vast expenses. ❧ I thought often of that little frog swimming with the scorpion on his back and wondered if I would suffer the same fate. Then it happened: Gary and I made a wrong business decision. The sting came swiftly. Our Dublin-based studio with its 400 employees crashed into financial ruin. Just as the vultures began circling to gobble up the remains and I was having thoughts of retiring to a monastery in Tibet, the phone rang. A voice said, "I'm Bill Mechanic, CEO of Twentieth Century Fox. I want to start an animation division. What do you say?" ❧ Bill demonstrated his creative and marketing skills at Disney a few years back, and he was rumored to be well acquainted with the perils of the labyrinth. I cowered, but suddenly Oscar pushed the words out of my mouth, "Love the idea, Bill; when do we start?" ❧ "Someone must be watching over us," I said to Gary as I clicked the phone onto the receiver. "We should have been toast by now; you must have a guardian angel. Anyway, I must tell you something," I said. "You know the last fifteen years you and I have been in the labyrinth making those seven pictures?" "Yes," Gary replied. "Well," I continued, "I think it was all just schooling. Our real moment in the sun is about to happen." ❧ In the months that followed the excitement of building Fox Animation Studios intensified. *Anastasia* was targeted as our first production as artists from fourteen countries arrived and settled in to meet the challenge. And in the days that followed the magnificent story of the lost princess became real. The movie burst upon our CinemaScope screen with shimmering colors, haunting melodies, and an emotional grandeur that swept me off my feet. "Wow," I said to Gary. "Are we really a part of making this? Really?" ❧ The cap on the wonderful journey of making *Anastasia* came while

I was in Los Angeles recording the score for the picture with composer David Newman. When I went down to breakfast at the hotel restaurant I found the assistant director, Jason, chatting with an elegant woman sitting with her teenage son, both strangers to us. I gathered he had let the cat out of the bag, for I heard her say, "Animation?" She stopped eating her oatmeal, and I was suddenly aware that she was staring at me. "I can tell by your face that you're creative," she said with a thick southern accent, drawing me in. She was suddenly standing beside us, smiling. "Please forgive me, but I have something to say to you." Oh, no. Here it comes, I thought. She's going to tell me that her son is an artist and wants to go to work for Fox. "God has given me purpose," she began. A seed caught in my throat. She smiled, "All the sacrifices you've made, all the hardships you've endured, all the difficulties you've encountered—all those trials are about to be rewarded." "This must be Gary's guardian angel," I mused. "What's she doing here at the Marriott?" "I'm here to tell you what you are doing is going to change the face of animation; brace yourselves, it's going to be big." From the corner of my eye I caught her son getting up to leave. "Come on, Mom." "Go on, I'll catch up," she returned. Once again our eyes locked. "There's one more thing I must say before I go," she said softly. Inside my head I heard the roll of drums. The sound you hear before the guillotine blade falls. "Please," I silently prayed, "don't say anything bad, no curses today." "Why do some people become so famous?" she began. "Cause God shines His light on them. His light is now going to shine on you. You're about to understand why you were born." Smiling, she touched my arm and vanished. ❧ Whether she was an honest-to-goodness oracle or just a kook, I'll never know, but either way, her words were encouraging, and I thought to myself, maybe this time the little frog will actually reach the other shore. ❧

Introduction by Gary Goldman

The motion picture *Anastasia* is a labor of love, dedication, and the conviction that a very special story could be created from one of the most prominent mysteries of our time. ⬥ At the beginning of any creative process, an artist must face a blank page, that first moment between thought and physical execution, that pause before one puts pencil to paper. Will the artist record his marks or words artfully? Will the artist communicate her thoughts clearly? ⬥ In January 1994, when Don and I accepted the offer to assist Twentieth Century Fox in starting up a new animation studio, we were going to face several blank pages. There were no artists, no technicians, no management, and no facility. While we were deciding on a location and reviewing the first 10,000 job applications, we were still deliberating what the studio's first film would be. Finally in October of 1994 it was agreed that we would begin production on a musical fantasy, a twentieth-century fairy tale about the lost Russian Grand Duchess Anastasia. ⬥ All of the tools we had listed to set up the animation studio were put on the back burner. Fox's technical and engineering gurus informed us that they were going to provide the latest available equipment and develop methods that would replace our archaic tools. They declared that they would drag us (kicking and screaming if necessary) into the twenty-first century. ⬥ The artists we have assembled represent fourteen countries, with the greatest number coming from America, Ireland, Canada, and the Philippines. Half of the 326-member crew of traditional animation artists, computer animators, engineers, and administrators are experienced, dedicated animation staffers. They have become the mentors of the young, talented, first-time artists from local colleges, international art schools, and animation schools, whose skills have grown immensely during their two and a half years on this very special project. ⬥ The endeavor has been a journey of discovery both technically and artistically. The challenge has been great, the efforts overwhelming. The crew has exhibited extreme sacrifice and dedication to achieve a new level of quality in animation art. ⬥ The project is digitally produced, from the hand-drawn visuals and voice recordings to every musical note and each individual sound effect. Digitally speaking, more than three million individual computer files make up this film. This includes all art from the animators' key drawings to the final special FX in-betweens, from original conceptual story sketches to final handpainted backgrounds. Computer technology has helped us enhance the artists' work and produce animation art never before possible. ⬥ The art was compiled on thousands of blank pages and brilliantly rendered in this film. Many examples are represented in this beautiful book, expertly authored by animation historian Harvey Deneroff. We hope you enjoy *The Art of Anastasia* as much as we have enjoyed creating the film. ⬥

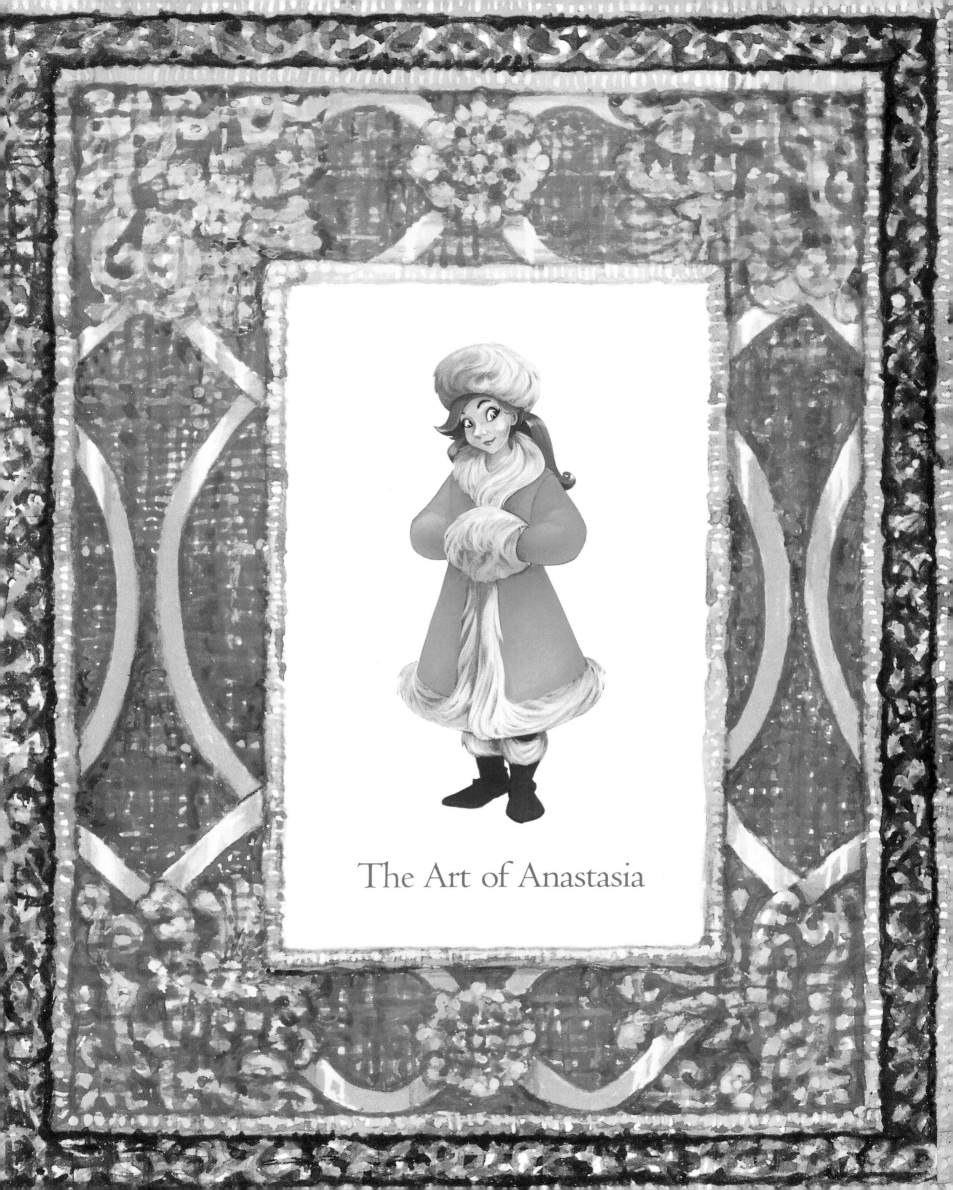

The Art of Anastasia

Chapter One

The Past Is Prologue

"The keys to your identity are found in the past. You must gather them up.
You will need them to unlock the doors to your future."

—DON BLUTH

❧

Anastasia began with a phone call—from Bill Mechanic, Fox Filmed Entertainment chairman and CEO, to coproducer and director Don Bluth. "Mechanic," Bluth recalls, "wanted to do something like *My Fair Lady*, where a girl is transformed from something ordinary to something quite glorious." This led them to consider a number of possible stories, including *Annie Get Your Gun*, "which was about this little country girl who becomes the star of Wild Bill Hickok's 'Wild West Show.' But soon we began asking 'How high could we go with this?' and the word 'princess' kept hitting the table, which got us to the story of Anastasia."

➤ Anastasia Nicholaievna was the youngest daughter of the last tsar and tsarina of Russia. In 1918, during the Russian Revolution, her parents and the her family were executed under a veil of secrecy. For several years afterward, rumors persisted that some or all of the family had survived, and various impostors emerged, claiming to be one or another of the tsar's children, including Anastasia. ➤ It was this tale that Fox Animation Studios turned to for inspiration in making its first animated feature film, produced and directed by Bluth and Gary Goldman. Although its parent company, Twentieth Century Fox, had previously produced a live-action version

Suzanne Lemieux Wilson's ancestral Romanov portraits are based on real paintings.

in 1956, starring Ingrid Bergman, the choice of this story as the basis of an animated film seems, at first glance, surprising.

The story overflows with romance and intrigue, but it is also, as Bluth admits, essentially "dark and tragic." Not exactly the usual subject matter for films designed for broad family audiences. Twentieth Century Fox had recently renewed its option on Marcelle Maurette's play *Anastasia*, on which the live-action film was based. In 1991, the remains of the tsar's family were exhumed, and Anastasia's body was found to be missing. With the mystery of Anastasia revived, Fox became interested in doing a new screen version, and the story also fit into Bluth and Goldman's desire

a film in CinemaScope, a wide-screen process not ordinarily used for animation. Goldman says, "We were excited about using the larger palette, which could fill the audience's eyes, and believed that the wide screen would also give it an epic quality." Fox, which had used the process for its earlier version of *Anastasia*, readily agreed. The result is a delightful, romantic musical comedy, which overlays the often harsh reality of its subject matter with some dazzling fairy-tale magic.

Bluth recalls, "We knew it had to be a guy and a gal on a journey, in which they discover who they are by their relationship to each other. We knew the theme was going to be Anastasia turning into some kind of a

fantastic princess, her male counterpart helping her get there, only to realize that he can have no part of it. All the pieces seemed to fit, so we began to explore it, and we pretty much knew, early on, that that was it."

"It was also apparent from the start," Bluth continues, "that the heroic journey in our story was a young girl's search for identity and family. The process of discovery is initiated by a journey into one's history. The keys to your identity are found in the past. You must gather them up . . . to unlock the doors in your future."

Executive producer Maureen Donley explains, "The real Anastasia was sixteen at the time of the revolution. However, we took her back to being a child, to see it through a child's eyes, so she would be someone kids could identify with. It also gives us a kismet thing between her and Dimitri, the kitchen boy—that they were soul mates and there was a destiny aspect at play. This change also brought into sharper focus the issue of 'finding home and what home means.' Is it a place or is it really more about the people you love and choose to spend your life with?" However, the main "through line," or theme, for Donley was "the fear of abandonment, which is one of the biggest fears kids have and which is something I don't think you ever lose as an adult. So, how do you deal with it, make peace with the past, and build a satisfying life for yourself?"

From the moment we first see the glittering Catherine Palace, the amazing scope of Anastasia *can be felt.*

A Special Gift. *Marie beckons to a young Anastasia during the celebration in order to give her a present.*
The music box plays a special song that Marie and Anastasia often sing together and it
unlocks with a key bearing the inscription "Together in Paris."

Various concept sketches of music boxes, keys, and royal furnishings were done before a final selection was made. Many of the pieces are based on actual belongings of the tsar's family.

The Romanovs

Nicholas II, Grand Duchess Anastasia's father, was the last tsar of Russia. His family, the House of Romanov, had ruled the country for more than three hundred years. Tsar Ivan the Terrible's first wife was, ironically, also named Anastasia. But it was Michael Romanov, her nephew, who began the Romanov Dynasty in 1613, when he was unanimously elected tsar by the Assembly of the Land, thus ending a turbulent period in Russian history known as the Time of the Troubles. The House of Romanov brought great glory and power to Russia but ultimately ended in tragedy.

The most well-known early Romanov tsar is Peter the Great, who, in his attempt to establish Russia as a European power, erected a new capital city, St. Petersburg, named after his patron saint. Construction began in 1703 on the Baltic Sea, near Russia's western border, and represented a new, westernized beginning for Russia. Designed by a cadre of French, Italian, Dutch, and German architects, St. Petersburg featured a series of magnificent palaces as grand as any found elsewhere in Europe.

Peter the Great's work in modernizing Russia and expanding its power was con-

Wilson's rendition of the Romanov children includes, from left to right;

Olga, Tatiana, Marie, Anastasia, and Alexei.

tinued by his successors, including Empress Catherine the Great. Although she realized in the late eighteenth century that the institution of serfdom, a form of slavery, needed to be reformed, along with Russia's autocratic system of government, it wasn't until 1861, during the reign of Alexander II, the Tsar Liberator, that the serfs were finally freed. Some democratic reforms were also considered,

but revolutionaries, frustrated at the slow pace of change, made several attempts on Alexander's life and finally succeeded in 1881.

Alexander III did not share his father's reformist views, and the assassination only confirmed his fear of such liberal policies. Afraid of dying himself at the hand of an assassin, he isolated himself and his family at their heavily guarded Gatchina estate and aban-

doned his father's democratic initiatives, a decision that would eventually lead to the end of tsarist rule.

Yet Alexander III's home life was a happy one. He enjoyed being a family man and truly loved his wife, Marie Feodorovna, the former Princess Dagmar of Denmark. It was no surprise that his son, Nicholas II, embraced the value of a strong family.

When young Nicholas fell in love with Princess Alice of Hesse-Darmstadt, granddaughter of Britain's Queen Victoria, their courtship was at first bitterly opposed by his parents, because Alice was part German. However, when Alexander III became seriously ill, he finally consented to their marriage, and Princess Alice became the Empress Alexandra. Nicholas was devoted to her and eventually came to rely on her political counsel. Nicholas and Alexandra had four daughters, Olga, Tatiana, Marie, and Anastasia, and a son, Alexis, the youngest and heir to the throne. Sadly, Alexis had hemophilia and was in constant danger of bleeding to death from even a minor injury. Alexandra's health declined after Alexis's birth and was not helped by the stress of caring for her sickly son. The only relief for them both came from Rasputin, a holy man, who miraculously seemed to be able to stop Alexis's bleeding episodes.

Nicholas had ascended to the throne in 1894 after his father's death, but he was unprepared to deal with the series of political crises that plagued Russia throughout his reign. Given only a limited military education, he was ill at ease in public and avoided close contact with his subjects. However, firmly believing in his God-given authority, Nicholas increasingly resisted pressures for political liberalization. After the disastrous Russo-Japanese War (1904–1905), which sparked an abortive 1905 revolution, Nicholas finally acceded to some long-sought reforms, including the creation of a Duma, or parliament. He subsequently tried to sabotage these initiatives, with considerable backing from the ruling aristocracy.

During this period, Rasputin began to exert more and more control over the course of government through Alexandra. His influence became even stronger during World War I, when Alexandra persuaded Nicholas to personally assume command of the Russian army, essentially leaving her and Rasputin to rule in his absence. (Rasputin and

Alexandra were later accused by some of being German spies.) The increasing concern over Rasputin's influence, expressed by the aristocracy and public alike, was ignored by Nicholas and Alexandra. In December 1916, when another governmental crisis saw the Duma dissolved, Rasputin was murdered by a group that included the tsar's nephew, Grand Duke Dmitri Pavlovich. (The conspirators eventually drowned him

through a hole in the ice, after attempts at poisoning and shooting him failed.)

Unaware of this intrigue, Nicholas never seemed to grasp the implications of this and other troubles that were besetting Russia. Finally, after rioting broke out in St. Petersburg in March 1917, the government collapsed. Nicholas, acceding to the demands of both the reconvened Duma and the army, stepped down as tsar. Initially, he abdicated in

favor of his brother Michael, rather than Alexis, but Michael refused the offer, thus ending the Russian monarchy.

The Duma established a provisional government and promised extensive democratic reforms. In the meantime, Nicholas and his family were interned at their summer palace, Tsarskoe Selo ("the tsar's village"), just south of Petrograd. In response to continuing revolutionary foment, the new government next sent them two thousand miles east to Tobolsk, in Siberia, postponing plans to send them to England.

Then, in November 1917, the Bolsheviks, led by V. I. Lenin, took power in a coup and signed a peace treaty in March 1918 with the Central Powers, including Germany. This angered their former WWI allies, including England, France, and the United States, who began to actively support the opposing faction in the ensuing civil war to depose the new communist government. In April 1918, the government transferred the imperial family to Ekaterinburg, in the Ural Mountains. When Ekaterinburg was in danger of being seized by the opposition, Lenin ordered the Romanovs' executions, which were carried out on the night of July 16, 1918.

This time the subject of Wilson's portrait is Nicholas himself.

The Prologue. *"I will not rest until I see the end of the Romanov line!"*

With these words, Rasputin's curse is issued—and the Romanovs' lives will never be the same again.

Anastasia: Myth and Reality

The fourth daughter of Tsar Nicholas II was born on June 18, 1901, into a life of extreme privilege and luxury.

Whatever Nicholas's failures as tsar, he and his wife, Alexandra, were loving and devoted parents. Like her sisters and brother, Anastasia had her own nursemaid and was educated by private tutors. Alexandra took a strong interest in her daughters' education and insisted that Anastasia and her sisters learn more than just how to play the piano and do needlework. In addition to Russian, the sisters also studied English, French, and German.

The family split its time among the Winter Palace in St. Petersburg, the Alexander Palace in Tsarskoe Selo ("tsar's village"), their summer home in Peterhof, and the Lividia Palace near Yalta, on the Black Sea. Every summer, they took an extended cruise on the imperial yacht, the *Standart*, in the Baltic Sea, off Finland.

Anastasia grew into a healthy, if somewhat overweight and mischievous, teenager, with reddish-blond hair. Possessing a quick wit, she loved playing practical jokes and was not above mimicking those around her, including official visitors. As a result, she earned the nickname of *Shvibzik*, or imp. She could also be very stubborn and had no interest in what others thought of her. It was said that she hardly ever cried, even when hurt.

Her idyllic life was changed somewhat by the outbreak of World War I, when her mother and two oldest sisters became nurses while she and her sister Marie frequently visited a nearby military hospital to cheer wounded soldiers. When her father abdicated in 1917, the family's life became more isolated and cloistered, but it wasn't until the provisional government sent them to Siberia in August 1917 that Anastasia's world was turned upside-down.

They stayed in the town of Tobolsk until May 1918, when the new Soviet government shipped them to the Ural town of Ekaterinburg. It was there that the Romanovs spent the last few months of their lives together before being gathered in a cellar room and executed on the night of July 16, 1918.

Because the Empress Alexandra was a German princess, and the Soviet government did not want to offend Germany, with whom they had just concluded a peace treaty, officials announced that only Nicholas had been killed and that the rest of the imperial family was safe. The Soviet government stuck by this story for a number of years, even hinting at one time that the family might have emigrated to America. It wasn't until 1924 that proof of what really happened was offered, and the results of an investigation were

Below: Anastasia demonstrates her mischievous personality with a little fun behind her father's back. Right: The figure in Wilson's portrait wears the costume of a "Boyar" (unmarried girl) but has a Romanov face.

published in Paris. However, Nicholas's mother, the Dowager Empress Marie, then living in Denmark, refused to accept its conclusions and steadfastly maintained until her death in 1928 that her son Nicholas and his wife and children were still alive.

Given these circumstances, it is not surprising that rumors started circulating soon after the executions that the imperial family had survived, or that pretenders surfaced, claiming to be one or another of Nicholas and Alexandra's children or grandchildren. But the story that would gain the most widespread attention started in Berlin in 1920, when a woman later identified as Anna Anderson tried to drown herself in the Landwehr Canal and was

taken to a mental asylum. There she said that she was the Grand Duchess Anastasia Nicholaievna and that she had escaped from Siberia to Romania with the help of a soldier, with whom she had a child that she later gave up. She had come to Berlin to see her aunt, Princess Irene of Prussia, but had lost her courage and thrown herself into the canal.

Anderson's claim elicited both fervent belief and vehement opposition from the Romanov family and others who had known Anastasia. The Dowager Empress, who might have confirmed or denied her identity, refused to see Anderson, apparently because she had given birth to an illegitimate child. Her

opponents suspected that Anna Anderson was only after the Romanov fortune, which was rumored to be in various European banks. Anderson continued to hold fast to her assertion until she died in the United States in 1984, leaving many to wonder who she really was.

In 1991, the remains of the imperial family were exhumed. DNA analysis clearly identified the bodies of Nicholas, Alexandra, and three of their children: Olga, Tatiana, and Marie. Those of the Grand Duchess Anastasia and the Tsarevitch Alexis, however, were not found. A similar analysis was later done on the remains of Anna Anderson, which clearly showed that she was not Anastasia. As a result, the mystery of Anastasia remains unsolved.

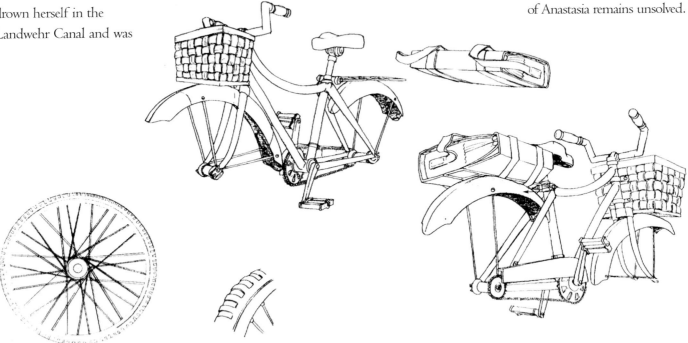

Left: This portrait of the Romanovs dancing in a field was based on an image from a Romanov family album.

The artists took great care to animate the props accurately. Above: A sketch of a period bicycle.

Separated! *A young Dimitri helps Anastasia and Marie escape from the palace under siege. The pair reach the train station only to lose each other when the train pulls away with only Marie onboard. Anastasia runs after her grandmother but slips and bumps her head.*

Anna Anderson on Stage, Screen, and Television

The story of Anna Anderson served as the inspiration for a number of plays, movies, and television dramas. The most popular fictional versions of the story were based on the French play *Anastasia* by Marcelle Maurette and its English-language adaptation by Guy Bolton, which became a hit Broadway show in 1954, starring Viveca Lindfors. The plot begins in Berlin in 1926 and involves an attempt by Prince Bounine to pass off Anna, a woman he saved from committing suicide, as the Grand Duchess Anastasia in order to gain a share of the Romanov fortune. Anna succeeds beyond Bounine's expectations in convincing the Dowager Empress, implying that she really is Anastasia. In the end, she leaves behind the people associated with her past to go off by herself, in the Dowager Empress's words, "To find life—her real life."

The play was first adapted into a film in 1956. This Twentieth Century Fox release was directed by Anatole Litvak and starred Ingrid Bergman as Anna, the role that marked her return to Hollywood; Yul Brynner as "General" Bounine; and

Helen Hayes as the Dowager Empress; with music by Alfred Newman. In 1967, a Hallmark Hall of Fame production on NBC-TV directed by George Schaeffer starred Julie Harris as Anna, and Lynn Fontanne, who came out of retirement to play the Dowager Empress. The first musical version of the play, *I, Anastasia*, was staged in Miami in 1982 and has no relation to the current animated version.

In 1956, *Anastasia—Die letzte Zarentochter* (*Anastasia—The Czar's Last Daughter*), also known as *Is Anna Anderson Anastasia?*, was released in Germany. Directed by Falk Harnack, it starred Lilli Palmer as Anna Anderson. Peter Kurth's popular book *Anastasia: The Riddle of Anna Anderson* (Little, Brown, 1983) was the basis of an American television miniseries directed by Marvin J. Chomsky, *Anastasia: The Mystery of Anna*, which featured an all-star cast, including Amy Irving as Anna, Olivia De Havilland as the Dowager Empress, and Rex Harrison as Grand Duke Cyril Romanov, with Omar Sharif and Claire Bloom as Nicholas and Alexandra.

Photographs of the real Anastasia in 1917 (above) and Anna Anderson in 1930 (right) reveal physical similarities.

What if you were the most beloved of children? Safe and warm in your family's arms and all the riches of the world at your disposal, then, in an instant, it all vanishes and you've lost everything—even your own identity. That was our hook into the story."

—MAUREEN DONLEY, EXECUTIVE PRODUCER

The Prologue

Anastasia's opening, like that of all fairy tales, sets up a conflict between good and evil; it also shows how the eight-year-old Anastasia's world collapses and she is suddenly left alone. As executive producer Maureen Donley puts it, "paradise and paradise lost."

The prologue's aim is to provide the story's background swiftly and clearly. To do this, the scriptwriters, Susan Gauthier and Bruce Graham—working with Don Bluth, Gary Goldman, Donley, lyricist Stephen Flaherty, and composer Lynn Ahrens—compress a series of historical events that actually took place between 1913 and 1918 into one night of terror. In addition, they introduce most of the main characters—Anastasia, the Dowager Empress Marie, a

ten-year-old Dimitri, Rasputin, and Bartok the bat—along with the film's two most important props, the music box and the reliquary. As Bluth notes, "That's a lot of stuff to get in the audience's mind, before you can say, 'Okay, now we're going to tell you a story.'"

To help convey the emotional overtones as clearly as possible, the directors placed a heavy emphasis on color. Bluth explains, "In a piece of music, the orchestration of the sounds becomes the thing that dictates the emotions of the moment. Colors do the same thing. So, as we work our way through a picture, we try to put our finger on, first of all, what is the emotional content of any moment in the movie? That emotional content dictates what the colors on the screen

should be, because different colors have different emotional or psychological impact."

In applying this method to the prologue, the sequence was broken down into five distinct sections, each with its own color scheme. "The first one," Bluth notes, "is celebrating the Romanov dynasty, and the secret that the grandmother and the little girl share—the music box and the locket around her neck, which bears an inscription promising they will be 'Together in Paris.' Here the images are warm reds and golden colors. Suddenly, Rasputin enters the great hall and everything changes from glorious to frightening, to bright, saturated reds, greens, and other raw colors suggesting revolution or war.

"Then there's the escape out

of the palace and onto the ice. The ice, of course, is very cold and the color scheme becomes gray and lifeless, because Rasputin's about to die. Then we go through the moment where Anastasia is knocked down at the train depot, bumps her head, and becomes unconscious. So, those colors have to have the same emotional impact: they're gray and dull, the colors that are depressing to us.

"So, after we put the audience through the trauma of Anastasia's great misfortune, about the only thing we can do in the next moment is come up for the title logo, where we are up in the clouds, and it's bright and sunny. Then we go right into the opening song, 'A Rumor in St. Petersburg.'"

The locket that Anastasia wears doubles as the key to the music box that Marie had given her.

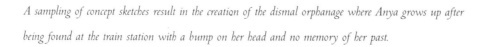

A sampling of concept sketches result in the creation of the dismal orphanage where Anya grows up after being found at the train station with a bump on her head and no memory of her past.

Chapter Two

Journey to St. Petersburg

Originally, the song "A Rumor in St. Petersburg" introduced all the characters and wound up repeating some of the information that the prologue provided. Therefore, it was shelved and Lynn Ahrens and Stephen Flaherty wrote another song as the film's opening number. Don Bluth describes it as "a little more imperial, pompous, and filled with pageantry. Then, we started thinking about starting the story off with the idea that there's a question that everyone is asking, Did the princess live or not? And just by singing that question, we actually advance the plot a long way. We meet Vladimir, we meet Dimitri, expose what their plan is, and we meet the new environment in Russia. We set a lot of the plot in motion, and at the same time tell what the story is going to be about with just one musical number." At this point, Kevin Bannerman notes, "We then reconceived, focused, and trimmed down 'Rumor' to give it its specific story thrust." ⬤ The scheme being hatched by the now twenty-year-old Dimitri and Vladimir, a former member of the imperial court, is to find a girl to pass off as Anastasia, in hopes of collecting a ten-million-ruble reward from her grandmother, who lives in Paris. ⬤ In sharp contrast to the large-scale, razzmatazz opening

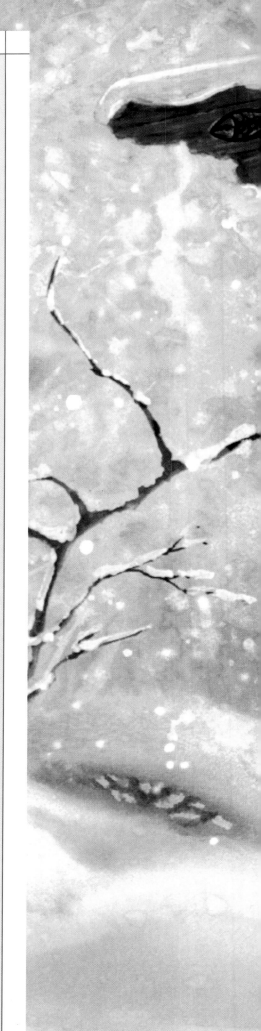

Anya at the Crossroads. *The path to the left leads to employment and remaining an orphan forever, to the right, St. Petersburg and the chance for a new future.*

number, which seems to involve practically everybody in St. Petersburg, the action switches to a quiet orphanage in the countryside. Here Anya, an eighteen-year-old orphan, has no memory or relics of her past, except for a locket with the inscription, "Together in Paris." She is leaving the orphanage, where she has lived for the past ten years, to go out on her own and take a job in a fish factory. She is in fact really Anastasia, but, as Bluth points out, Anya will have to undertake "a journey of discovery before she can find out who she is."

Her quest begins when she reaches a crossroads and prays for guidance, which appears in the form of Pooka, a little dog who, to Bluth, "represents her guardian angel. It is 'a little child shall lead them' theme." Following Pooka's advice,

Anya forsakes her job and goes to St. Petersburg. Her thoughts and hopes are expressed in "Journey to the Past," in which she sings, "Let this road be mine! Let it lead me to my past and bring me home . . . at last!" For Bluth, the decision Anya makes here relates to what the film is all about: "the choices one makes in life's journey." Once in St. Petersburg, Anya finds that she needs an exit visa to get to Paris and is told to seek out Dimitri as someone who might help her. She arrives at the abandoned, boarded-up palace, where Dimitri and Vlad are secretly staying. Not knowing where else to go, she breaks in and comes upon the ruins of the ballroom, where several items, including a painting of the Romanov family, seem to her "like a memory from a dream."

To the tune of the lullaby her grandmother sang in the prologue, she sings "Once Upon a December," as royal ghosts step out of the portraits and waltz around her. ➤ Her reverie is broken by Dimitri and Vlad, who realize Anya is perfect for the part of Anastasia. Without telling her of their plan, Dimitri convinces her to go to Paris with them to see if she might be the real Anastasia. Bluth points out, "When Anya and Dimitri meet, the ballroom is ice cold, and the walls are a gray-green. The colors feel cool, not ardent, warm, or passionate, because both of them are being very cold to each other, holding back, not saying what they're really feeling." ➤ Their conversation is overheard in the rafters by Bartok, the albino bat who was once Rasputin's sidekick.

He believes Anastasia is dead, but Anya's voice stirs the minions in Rasputin's reliquary, who drag Bartok down to limbo, where Rasputin has been stuck since he died. The bright neon green glow of the reliquary evokes Rasputin's entrance in the prologue, and the scene is played for broke with off-the-wall slapstick. Rasputin complains, "Look at me. I'm falling apart," as various body parts, including a hand and his lips, take on lives of their own. Yet, as Bluth points out, Rasputin's villainy remains undiminished as he marches off, singing "In the Dark of the Night," in which he exhorts, "Come, my minions, rise for your master, let your evil shine," preparing to kill Anastasia once and for all. ➤

"A Rumor in St. Petersburg." *Townsfolk dance while Dimitri and Vladimir concoct a scheme during this lively musical number.*

The song quickly sets up the concurrent climate in the city and gives the audience a sense that something big is about to happen.

A Matter of Style

Even though the script was specifically tailored for the animation medium, the subject matter presented an inherent challenge in both its historic backdrop and its necessary dependence on human characters. Paradoxically, this also ended up being one of the project's strengths. Gary Goldman recalls, "We kept saying, 'It's live action. It's live action.' Then we asked ourselves, 'If it's going to be animation, what can we do to make it acceptable?'" They decided that to make it work, they would need to, as Goldman says, "push for reality in the animation to bring it to life."

The "push for reality" extended to all aspects of the film, including exterior and interior settings. Layout department head Phil Cruden rejected numerous conceptual drawings because the artist had "not used any reference" to photos of actual locales. Although the untrained eye might not be able to detect the difference, the film's use of authentic details lends it a credibility that makes the supernatural aspects, as well as the big musical numbers, all the more effective.

All the character animators who worked on the film were keenly aware that *Anastasia* was an animated film, not a live-action one. Goldman notes, "Humans are the hardest characters for animators to draw. Audiences are very familiar with the way the human body moves, and if you move it oddly, or don't draw it well, it's easily criticized." With that in mind, animators worked closely with live-action reference footage.

The footage was videotaped under the direction of Don Bluth, who staged the action on a bare-bones set, using props and costumes that were more suggestive than realistic. This kept the focus of attention on the actors and their movements. Then the individual frames of the videotape were blown up into stills and given to the animators.

A temptation in this sort of process is to copy, or roto-scope, each actor's every move. However, as directing animator Len Simon notes, "If you just trace the stats, the characters seem floaty, like they're walking underwater. What a good animator does is use the stats as a guide, along with the performance provided by the voice actors and the design of the character, to create a credible animated performance all its own. A lot of people just take for granted that some scene is rotoscoped. But most of the time, the final result is nothing like the original stats." Thus, the film's realism is more the reflection of an artistic vision than of an effort to make a reality-based documentary.

The layout department uses reference photos to sketch the authentic interior settings. Similarly, animators rely on live-action footage of actors to study how the human body moves and reacts.

Anya Meets Pooka. *In Pooka, Anya discovers not only a sign to go to St. Petersburg but also a true friend.*
Above, top to bottom: After her meeting with Pooka, Anya finds out at the ticket window that getting to Paris
will not be so easy. She will find help in the unlikely forms of Dimitri and Vladimir.

Anya

Gary Goldman recalls that Anya started to take shape when "Bill Mechanic said he would like to use Meg Ryan's voice. Don had been developing her design and character for about three months, without success. So he finally grabbed a snippet of Meg's voice from *Sleepless in Seattle* and animated three scenes in continuity himself, to show Bill what she might look like."

"We then went to Meg," Don Bluth recalls, "and showed her the test, which she liked a lot. Then, as we began recording the lines, we noticed that her voice has a rough edge to it. She's very spirited, but it was not your typical, saccharine heroine voice. So, I went back to the drawings and kind of roughed them up a bit. She still had a very beautiful face, but not overly made up. Her hair was sort of disheveled and deliberately messy; even her clothes don't fit her very well."

Goldman also notes, "Don gave the character an Audrey Hepburn kind of heart-shaped face, with very pronounced eyebrows and almond-shaped eyes. So if you put your hand across the middle of Anya's face, you've got Meg Ryan on the bottom, with Meg's messy hair, and this kind of a classical look around the eyes. Putting her hair up and tying it in a knot

also allowed us to later drop her hair down, so we can see her femininity." This is just one aspect of Anya's Pygmalion-style transformation, which is also seen in her costumes, "going from ragamuffin orphan in a hand-me-down smock to someone who's decked out like a full princess."

Her transformation, Bluth says, is also apparent in her voice. "You can hear in her later lines, when she's realizing more and more what her heritage really is. She begins to talk a little differently. It's still Meg. She still has the fight, and she will not let anybody put her down, but at the same time she becomes quite a lady."

Standard Anya is 6 1/2 heads tall

Animators follow certain guidelines to ensure that each character's appearance is consistent throughout the film. Right: This sampling shows only some of the specifications that Anastasia animators adhere to.

Head construction

Head and shoulders turn

Avoid "fingers" + equal separation of hair

to "group" hair elements

Animators use a dancers gestures with hands

Audrey Hepburn eyes

Hair part centered above Anya's eyes

Avoid spreading all fingers
and getting equal positive and
negative shapes. I.e., All fingers
spread or all spread apart the
same distance.

Action

Action

"Drag" on sleeve

Action

"Drag"

Action

Avoid parallel lines in your design

Incorrect

Correct

"M," "P," or "B"   "EH" or A   "U" (OO)

"AH"   "S" or "EE"   "O" (OH)

Left: A Wilson portrait of a young Anastasia is surrounded by the many faces of Anya, from young girl to ragamuffin orphan to royalty.

Pooka

Anya's dog, Pooka, who is a sort of a Jiminy Cricket character, initially also proved troublesome, but for different reasons. "Originally," Don Bluth recalls, "it was going to be a ferret, and then it was going to be a mink, and then at one point a rat! Finally we said, 'Oh, come on, let's do something soft and cuddly, something that she could really like. We were trying to be different, which is not really always the honest way to go. In the end, having this little puppy dog come up to her seemed to be the most natural."

It also tends to make Pooka's symbolism as a guardian angel a little less obvious. Thus, having a dog crawl into the old palace before Anya or barking at Rasputin's minions outside the train before anyone else sees them fits in with most people's perception of how dogs behave.

There were frustrations doing Pooka's voice. "We couldn't get a human to do it," Gary Goldman says. "We tried several expert voice artists. They didn't sound doglike enough. Instead, we recorded about sixteen different dogs," then edited them together to create Pooka's distinctive barks, growls, and various moans to assimilate a personality.

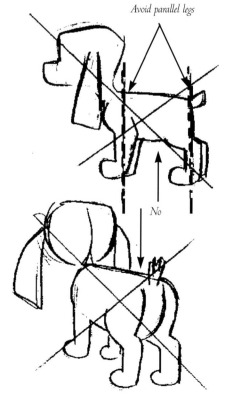

Avoid parallel legs

No

Do this instead

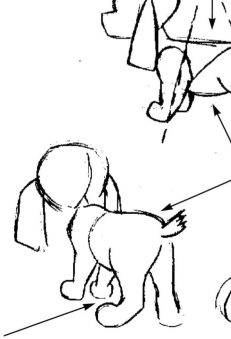

Do this instead

Yes

Front paw

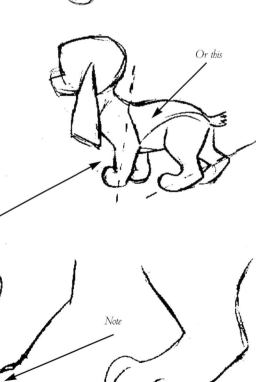

Or this

Note

Hind paw

Paw underside

Pooka's lively personality emerges with the aid of directionals provided at the beginning of the animation process. Below: A regal Pooka demonstrates the preferred dog stance.

The Palace. *Anya looks for Dimitri at the abandoned palace and almost instantly feels a sense of déjà vu. Above: The subjects of royal family portraits dance through the air in a magical waltz.*

The Connection. *Anya imagines being with her forgotten sisters and father in the old, deserted ballroom. Dimitri and Vladimir hatch a plan on the spot after noticing Anya's obvious resemblance to the princess Anastasia in the family portrait.*

Anatomy of a Frame: Bartok and the Reliquary

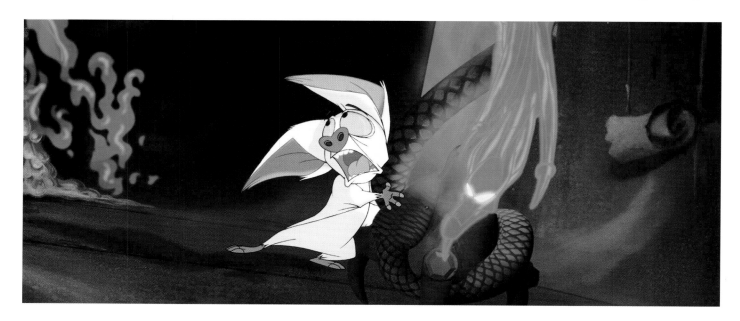

As Anya agrees to accompany Dimitri and Vladimir to Paris, their voices carry up to the rafters of the palace ballroom where Bartok the bat, Rasputin's old sidekick, overhears them. In a dry, matter-of-fact tone, Bartok says (to no one in particular), "Anastasia. Yeah, just one problem there fella—Anastasia's dead. All the Romanovs are dead. They're dead, dead, dead, dead."

Behind him, the reliquary, the source of all Rasputin's power, is coming to life, with its distinctive neon green glow. Wisps of smoke flow ominously from the top, minions pour forth, and Bartok realizes, "If that thing's come back to life it must mean Anastasia's alive . . ."

The setting for this shot began in the layout department with the initial sketch. The art was then turned over to the background department to be finished and painted based on a color model. Meanwhile, the animation department provided the drawings of Bartok to use throughout the scene.

As was every other prop, the reliquary was initially designed in the layout department. However, because of the reliquary's special attributes, it was then forwarded to the computer animation department, which turned it into a computer-generated object. It was finally brought to life with the green gaseous substance that it emits.

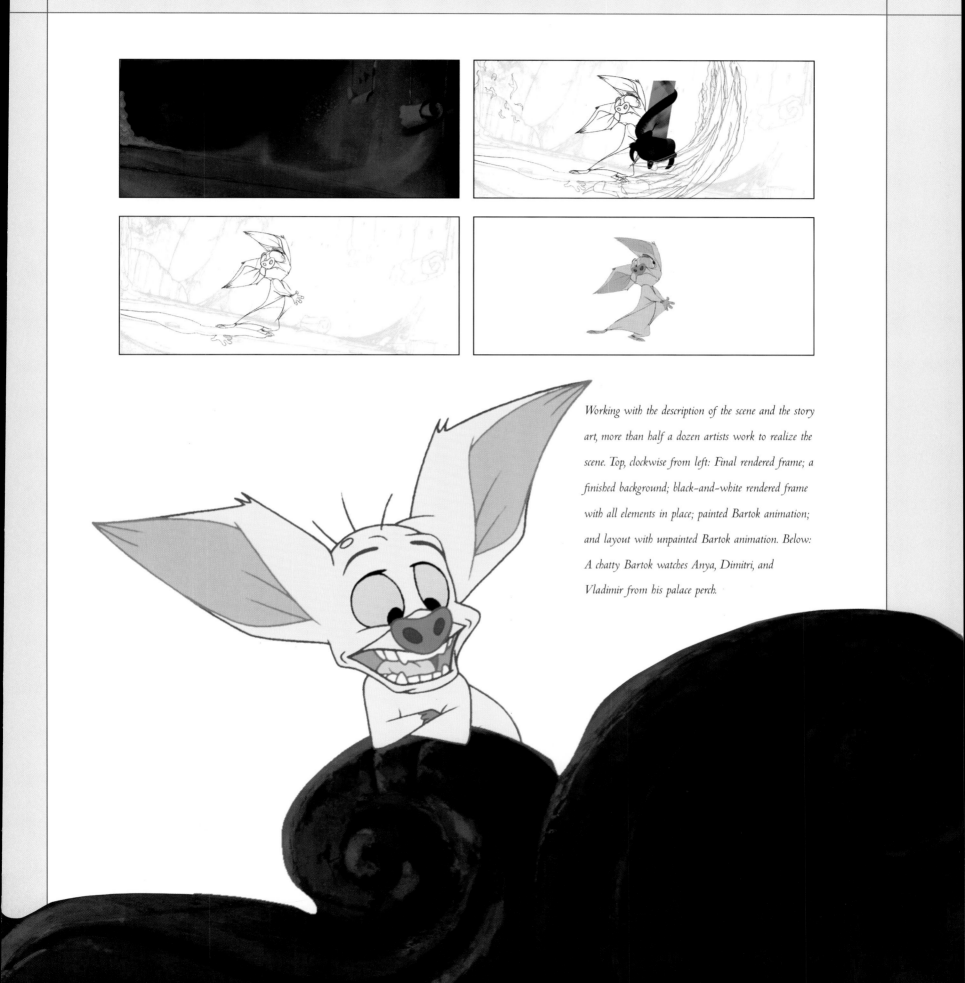

Working with the description of the scene and the story art, more than half a dozen artists work to realize the scene. Top, clockwise from left: Final rendered frame; a finished background; black-and-white rendered frame with all elements in place; painted Bartok animation; and layout with unpainted Bartok animation. Below: A chatty Bartok watches Anya, Dimitri, and Vladimir from his palace perch.

As one of the most important—and certainly the most animated—props, the reliquary undergoes many designs before the ominous skull (right) is selected.

Concept art for Rasputin's dwellings focuses on the surreal and spooky. None of these selections made it past the drawing board, but they demonstrate the tremendous range of possibilities, from the nearly Seuss-like to the macabre pillars of skeletons.

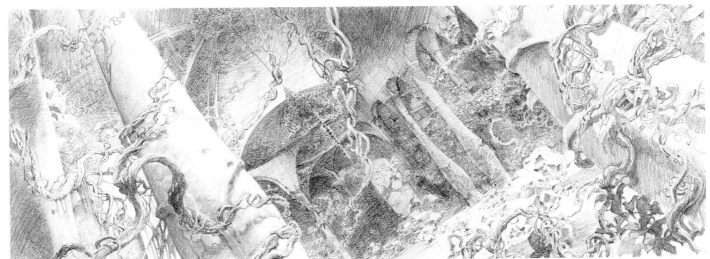

Painters rely on color keys while they work to ensure consistency. These color keys show Rasputin in limbo reunited with Bartok and the reliquary.

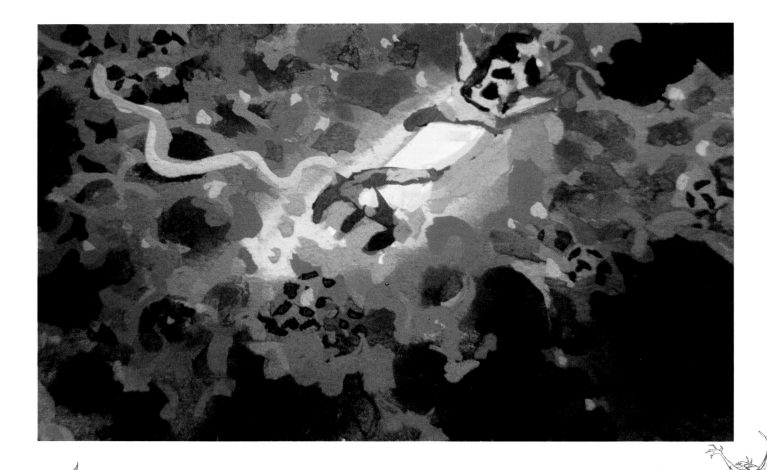

Creating Multitudes of Characters

"A Rumor in St. Petersburg," the elaborate opening production number, with its large ensemble, is one of the reasons why Goldman calls *Anastasia* "an incredible scene planning nightmare." Without digital technology, this and many other scenes would have been impossible or too expensive to do.

One of the traditional problems animators have faced is the limited number of levels on which actions can take place. The physical limitations inherent in celluloids, or cels, on which character were inked, painted, and then laid over the background, usually precluded the use of more than four or five cel levels, lest color values change and images be lost. With computers, an unlimited number of levels are possible without any loss of color or image.

Computers also make it possible to multiply a few characters into a huge crowd. For example, in *The Lion King*, the wildebeest stampede was actually created by manipulating the animation of a single animal. A similar approach was used in *Anastasia* for several scenes of much greater complexity.

Directing animator Troy Saleba recalls, "We might animate twenty-five characters in a scene, but with the computer we were able to multiply them into hundreds. For 'A Rumor in St. Petersburg,' they multiplied characters like crazy. It would have been ridiculous to do by hand. We would have done something that was more of a cheat, where you would not see the individual characters. There would just have been some shapes off in the distance."

While the crowd scenes in the "St. Petersburg" number used up to two hundred levels, directing animator John Hill points out that there were in excess of "nine hundred levels in one shot in the 'In the Dark of the Night' number, where there are hundreds of bugs everywhere!"

Technology, however, does not necessarily make these scenes easy to pull off. As Goldman says, "The trick is distributing the characters appropriately. We need to be able to fill the screen with a crowd and color them so you will not really be aware that we're reusing elements."

The impressive attention to detail throughout the film is readily evident in Marie's carriage. In addition to the use of the actual royal crest and its authentic design, the 3-D department later adds texture maps to several surfaces, like the cushions, for a richer result.

The Catherine Palace Ballroom

The settings in *Anastasia* play a key role in the story, especially those that re-create the splendor of Imperial Russia and of Paris in the 1920s. The layout department was responsible for designing the film's architectural settings; in other words, providing the acting space in which the characters play out their roles.

In reconstructing St. Petersburg for the film, the layout department relied on contemporary photographs in books, as well as photos and videotapes taken on location by Gary Goldman. In all, Goldman took 3,600 still photos and ten rolls of videotape of the city, some from a helicopter. He also visited all the possible Russian locations that might be used in the movie, much as a location scout does for a live-action film.

Based on this material, the layout artists were able to reconstruct the landscape of St. Petersburg and do preliminary drawings, or conceptual art, of the various settings. For instance, the original script specified that the ballroom of the Winter Palace be used in the prologue and later scenes, including the "Once Upon a December" dream waltz. It was with these layouts that one of the first animation tests was done with Anya. However, the tests proved the setting to be unsatisfactory, and it was decided to use the more spacious ballroom of the Catherine Palace in Tsarskoe Selo instead.

Though the new setting was more promising, it still seemed too cramped. Goldman notes, "The ceiling was too low and flat, so we decided to enlarge it." The ceiling was elevated and given a more arched appearance. The ballroom was lowered from the second floor to the first, effectively doubling its height, and was made more dramatic by providing a grand staircase on which guests would descend to the dance floor.

The actual ballroom is decorated with large mirrors,

which are used to great effect in the prologue to intensify the golden glow of the opening shots of the Romanov tricentennial celebration, along with appropriate furniture, including several thrones. In addition, conceptual artist Suzanne Lemieux Wilson provided paintings of the imperial family and the Russian aristocracy that were digitally "mapped" on the walls so they would not have to be redrawn each time the camera angle changed.

Aside from making the appropriate changes to evoke the room's disrepair ten years after the revolution, the layouts were then transformed by the color key and background departments to be readied for production.

The ballroom is impressive even as a sketch (right).

Below: The background for the ballroom showcases its splendor.

Chapter Three

By Land and Sea

he middle section of *Anastasia* follows Rasputin's renewed vow to kill the last of the Romanovs. Here the film turns into a full-blown romantic adventure, complete with feats of derring-do, last-minute rescues, and the first stirrings of romance between Anya and Dimitri. The section's two big action sequences—the train wreck and the nightmare at sea—include the movie's most extensive use of computer-generated, three-dimensional environments, seamlessly blended with hand-drawn elements to provide a heightened sense of realism and danger. Accompanying all this is the beginning of Anya's transformation from ragamuffin orphan to princess and the emergence of a subplot involving Vladimir's long-held affection for Sophie, the Empress Marie's cousin and lady-in-waiting. On a train heading out of St. Petersburg, Dimitri, Vladimir, and Anya have embarked on the first leg of their trip to Paris, armed with exit visas that Vlad has forged. When he realizes that these papers are no good, the three-

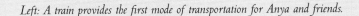

Left: A train provides the first mode of transportation for Anya and friends.

some flees to the baggage car, only to find themselves trapped by Rasputin's minions. Thanks in part to Anya, they escape certain death as the train crashes and explodes, leaving Dimitri with a newfound respect for her. On their way to the boat for the final leg of their journey, Dimitri and Vladimir teach Anya about Anastasia with the song "Learn to Do It," described in the script as "the Pygmalion song." Anya seems to learn her lessons well, even mentioning, to Dimitri and Vladimir's surprise, a fact that neither of them "believe we told her." Anya's beauty

is revealed for the first time when she puts on a newly recycled blue dress for a waltz lesson. Dimitri and Anya dance while Vladimir sings the "Waltz Revise of 'Learn to Do It.'" in which he laments what is happening between Anya and Dimitri, noting, "I taught her well. I planned it all! I just forgot . . . romance!" Don Bluth points out that in this scene, "neither Dimitri nor Anya are able to express their love for one another. I knew we needed soft colors, pastels, that would be in the pinks, which we put in the sky in the form of a sunset. The colors in the sky do not remain

the same, but go through five different changes as you watch this little dance: golden colors into more orange colors, into the pinks, and finally into the darker colors, like the maroons, as the sunset deepens. Even the shading on their faces is saying that this is an intimate moment filled with a certain kind of excitement. But at the same time, we are seeing young love, very nervous, and extremely beautiful. It's a good feeling." — That night, in their cabin, Anya's memories are further stirred, first by seeing the music box, which she thinks has "something to do with a secret," and later by sleepwalking. As she dreams, Rasputin's minions invoke the idyllic life of her imperial childhood to lure her onto the ship's storm-drenched deck in an attempt to drown her, and Dimitri saves her just in the nick of time. As she comes to, Anya mutters something about "the Romanov curse," the meaning of which neither understands. — Frustrated by the failures of his minions to kill Anya, Rasputin realizes that he will "have to kill her myself. In person," and takes off for the surface of the earth for a final confrontation in Paris. —

The train ride begins peacefully enough, but the tension quickly mounts. From top to bottom: Vladimir makes fast friends with Pooka; Vladimir is about to realize that his phony passports won't work; and Pooka barks an alarm.

Pooka is the first member of the group to come face-to-face with one of Rasputin's minions (below).

Right: Additional dangers manifest in a luggage car stocked with explosives and an engine furnace burning too hot.

Rasputin and Bartok

Once it was decided that Rasputin would be the villain, neither his final design or finding the right voice for him came easy. "I got photographs of him," Don Bluth recalls, "and I just started drawing pictures of this guy, at first realistic, then gradually caricatured, pushing further and further and further."

"If you look at him," he notes, "Rasputin is a real character, with his wizened hair pulled back in kind of a ponytail. Although it would seem easy to caricature him, we actually went through about a year of design work. Tom Steisinger, one of our young animators, must have done twenty-five or thirty really strong designs before we were satisfied.

"Originally, we avoided putting him in monk's clothes and had him in the type of robe that a villain would wear. But we thought, as long as we're going to say he *was* a holy man in the script, let's put him in a monk's outfit, so that he has a duality. He looks like a monk, but he certainly doesn't act like one."

Bluth further notes that Rasputin's reliquary evolved "when we realized he needed something that represented his power, the gun he wears

around his hip that he can still fire, that makes him lethal, even though he's dead. And because you can't kill a dead man, we had to give him an Achilles heel. If you hurt that, you hurt him."

Part of the reason it took so long to find a voice for Rasputin, Bluth concedes, "stemmed from the fact that we didn't know how comic he was going to be." After considering a number of actors we found out that Christopher Lloyd, who we knew could certainly play a villainous part, was available. I said, 'Let's go in and take some samples and see

if we can't make it work to some animation.' At the recording session, I threw him the three personalities that live within the skin of Rasputin. The first is the boisterous opera singer: a bombastic, loud, bellowing guy making demands. Then there's the sniveling, whimpering, self-pitying guy, who feels sorry for himself. The third is much more sinister: the sly, stalking predator, who tries to figure out how to get somebody. Lloyd seemed to be able to flip in and out of those with a lot of schizophrenia. So we said, 'There's the guy to go with.' "

Directing animator Len Simon, who had primary responsibility for Rasputin, says, "If you watch Christopher Lloyd act, he really doesn't do a lot. It's just the look he has, and those little shakes and stuff. With animation, you have to move him around a bit more, and get more out of the character. But Lloyd has a real interesting face and a presence. So, in animating Rasputin I tried to capture that presence."

The last major character to be added in the film was Rasputin's sidekick and comic straight man, Bartok the bat. As Gary Goldman says, "Every time you see a villain, they've always got a crow or parrot on their shoulder."

Bluth concurs, adding, "We asked, 'What can we do about this character that would make it different?' Bats have certainly been used many times, but not an albino bat. And then—we finally stumbled onto this—a bat who is very deadpan about everything, and not entirely in synch with his master. He keeps saying, 'Hey, take it easy. This is not good!' And at the end of the movie, Bartok says, 'You're on your own here, sir. I can't do this!' and leaves. He isn't quite the allegiant adjutant you would expect."

"Bartok," Bluth feels, "was the hardest voice in the whole picture. We originally had Martin Short record the voice. He gave an absolutely delightful performance, and we even animated some of it. Short, however, was shooting *Mars Attacks* at the same time and Fox's tight production deadlines necessitated continuing the search for the perfect Bartok. We finally discovered Hank Azaria. Then the whole thing sort of spun on a dime and we redesigned the character." Hank gave Bartok a laid-back air "and really defined the character," Donley adds.

Goldman remembers that he initially "didn't like Hank Azaria's readings. Then I heard it laid next to Christopher Lloyd's voice, and it really clicked. It provided a nice contrast, because one was just so laid back and the other was so manic."

John Hill, the directing animator who handled Bartok, really enjoyed animating him, since "he was more of a traditional animated cartoon character." Because there was little live-action reference footage shot, Hill basically relied on Bluth's original design, Azaria's voice, and his own ideas to do Bartok. "And," he adds, "Bartok has these very dry, reserved lines, which I like, because I'm a very laid-back kind of guy myself."

Rasputin's face is a compilation of exaggerated features and expressions that communicate his three main personalities: clamorous, self-pitying, and evil.

This amusing array of Bartok sketches demonstrate the albino bat's personality, whether he's holding a heavy reliquary, playing a game of golf, or juggling a new baby bat.

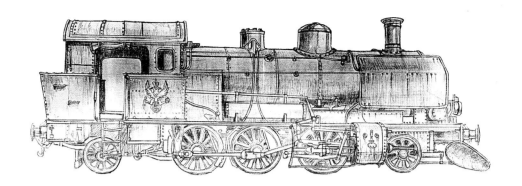

Top and bottom: These original drawings for a German locomotive were
supplied as 3-D models. Middle: The minions separate the baggage car from
the passenger car. Right: The original concept art for the bridge and gorge.

Animation Meets Technology: The Train Wreck

The action sequence aboard the train, in which Anya, Dimitri, and Vladimir confront Rasputin's minions, is staged very much like a live-action movie, complete with a panoply of digital objects and effects. Computers were used to build and then destroy the engine, coal tender, and baggage car where the action takes place, as well as to provide many incidental details that give the scene greater credibility.

Once in the baggage car, the three find themselves on a runaway train, because the minions have uncoupled it from the passenger cars. When Dimitri discovers there is no one driving the engine, he uses some dynamite that Anya has found to uncouple the baggage car from the coal tender, but this and other efforts fail to stop the car from hurtling toward a bridge that has been blown up by the minions.

Tom Miller, the film's digital imagery supervisor, describes what happens next. "They come up with a scheme to tie one end of a chain to the bottom of the chassis and throw the other end, with a grappling hook attached to it, onto the tracks in an attempt to stop the car. Unfortunately, all it does is yank out the chassis, which throws the car off the tracks sideways, careening toward the edge of the gorge. At this point, they have to

make a decision to jump or not. So with Anya saying, a little tongue-in-cheek, 'Well, this is our stop,' they all jump. At which point, we have a very exciting shot of the engine and coal car careening off the trestle, into the camera, while above you see the baggage car sliding sideways. The next shot looks down as the engine and

the coal car crash and explode; after this initial explosion, the baggage car, which is full of dynamite, follows and crashes on top of the engine and coal car, for a double explosion, with all this colorful smoke rising up to camera."

In this sequence, not only is the train computer generated, but much of the landscape and

the lighting effects are as well. In using digital technology, Miller took special care to create images that looked and felt as if they were drawn by hand and used hand-drawn elements skillfully grafted onto computer elements. For instance, after he constructed the baggage car on a computer using standard wire-frame tech-

niques, he "tiled on" a painted surface prepared by the background department. As Rob Nason, head of the background department, notes, "Applying our flat textures to the wire frame is what gives it a hand-painted look, because it is a hand-painted texture mapping that is 'tiled' on." In addition to providing hand-painted

surfaces, the texture mapping process was also used to "create a weathered look, where the surface seems pitted and decayed."

On top of all this, Miller realized that he could make the trains look more hand-drawn by superimposing wire-frame lines on top of the fin-ished train. These lines essen-tially replicate the inked lines used in cel animation, thus further blurring the lines between traditional and digital techniques.

It is with the explosions that the advantages of these new techniques become readily apparent. "In these shots we used UV texture mapping," Miller says, "which involves a one-to-one mapping onto the surface; therefore, when the [computer-generated] train explodes, the mappings stay with those pieces as they blast apart."

At times, computer-gener-ated elements were essentially used as a reference, much in the way live-action footage of actors is used by character animators. Thus, Miller initially created the climactic explosions digital-ly, then turned them over to the special-effects animators. The process saved time and provid-ed the appropriate graphic look the scene demanded.

"However," Miller points out, "the smoke pumping out of the engine was done entirely with the Softimage Particle System. The advantage here is that we were able to change the color of the smoke particles over time. So, we got a red firing smoke, which turns to black as it leaves the locomotive. In the past, one would need to take a series of multiple exposures to create the same look. Here we were able to do it all at once."

Other elements added by Miller and his colleagues are perhaps even less obvious, but no less important in building the sequence's cumulative effect. These include the lights the train throws down on various surfaces, even digitally created ones, creating the illusion of dimensionality on a flat, painted snowy ground. Miller's crew also made the baggage car's sideways plunge through the snow more credible by carefully "building up snow on the car itself, so it didn't feel so out of place."

Blending all these elements seamlessly is not an easy task, even with the latest in digital technology. Nevertheless, the range of traditional animation will continue to grow in new and exciting ways.

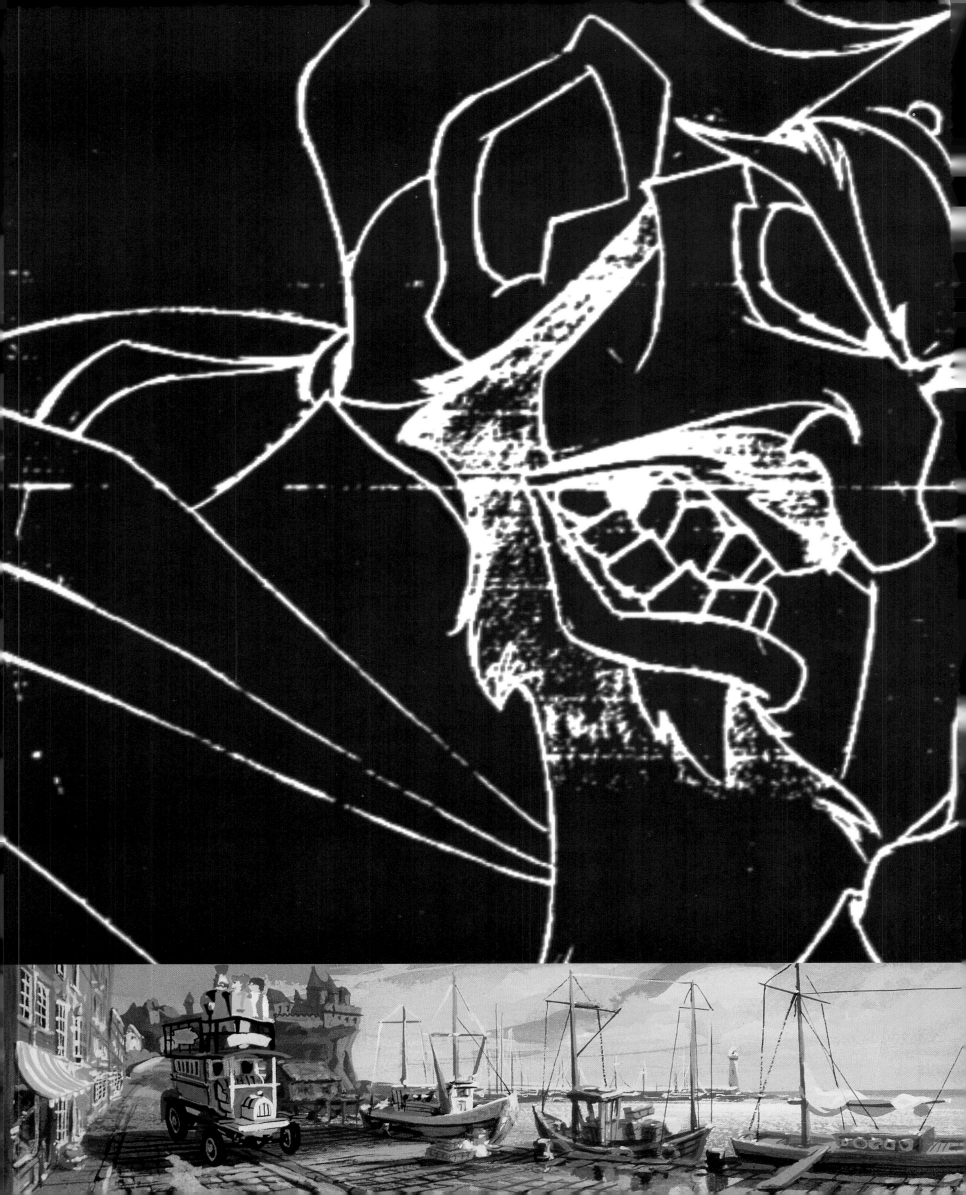

This negative provides an interesting glimpse of the reliquary before the 3-D department is put to work. Below: a color key of the festive seaside with our heroes en route to the boat that will carry them the rest of the way to Paris.

Learning to Be Royalty. *From top to bottom: Dimitri and Vladimir coach Anya on the details of a Romanov past; Vladimir becomes aware of the growing feelings between Dimitri and Anya while watching them waltz; Pooka discovers the music box that Dimitri retrieved as a young boy when Anastasia dropped it during her escape from the palace.*

Dimitri and Vladimir

Of all the characters in *Anastasia*, Don Bluth most admires Dimitri, because in the end he's the most heroic. "As a young boy," Bluth notes, "he had no money and was a kitchen boy in the palace. He watched the parties and luxury of the imperial court but was never part of it. As he grows up, he hatches schemes to make money and he becomes a pretty good con man. He's always enthusiastic but doesn't have a great deal of morality. But along the way he changes."

At first Bluth took the easy route in designing Dimitri and gave "him the ideal Sears Roebuck catalog look, with the perfect face, nose, and cheekbones. Then Bill Mechanic came into play; because I drew so many Dimitris, I grew weary of him. He said, 'Let's make a guy that's not very good-looking, just an everyday guy.' So we broke his nose a little bit, and took his hair and let it hang down any old way, so it gets kind of messy.

"The first Dimitris were also a little beefy. Bill said, 'No. No muscles on the guy. Let's keep him pretty ordinary. So we took all the muscles off of him. What he has to do is function with his brain. And,

oddly enough, judging by the reactions at the previews, by taking off all of those sexual kinds of physical affectations we created a very sexy guy. Which I don't quite get."

Once John Cusack's voice was recorded, Bluth adds, "Dimitri had to get tweaked again. In many cases, the voice you use becomes almost over-powering, and if it doesn't sound like it matches the character design, then you have to alter the design.

"Cusack, we knew, was a bit casual. So we rolled up Dimitri's sleeves, which gives us a chance to see a little bit of his arm. This makes him seem more youthful and it also gives the impression that he means business. You know, he's a busy guy, like a news-paper reporter that's sitting there, sweating it out."

Dimitri's partner in crime is Vladimir, voiced by Kelsey Grammer. A former member of the imperial court, Vladimir is an aristocrat who, despite being broke and rather overweight, retains his old military bearing. Bluth points out, "Vlad knows who was who and what's politically correct. He's the teacher, Dimitri is the schemer. But Vlad is a good character, and when Kelsey Grammer's voice came

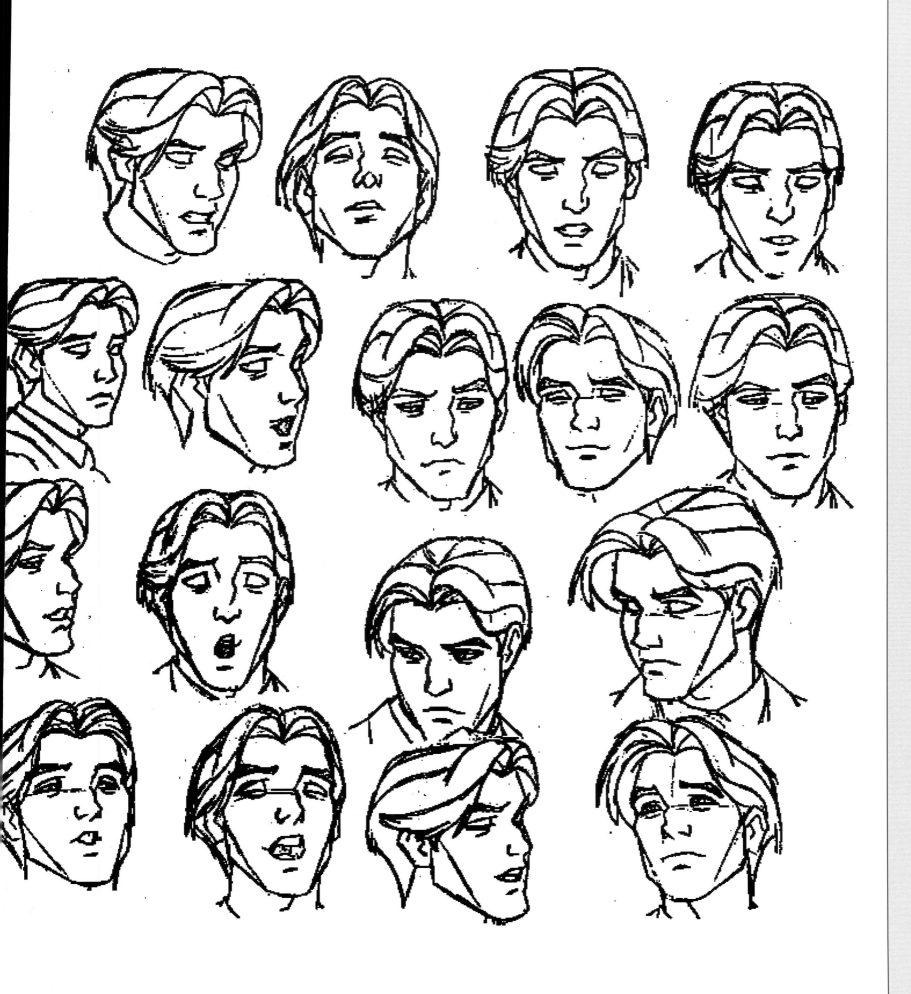

into it, it fit in pretty easily. I had some character designs on Vlad, and knew he was going to be kind of a hefty, fat guy, because we needed that for contrast."

Grammer, as Gary Goldman puts it, "is no fat guy, but he's got a big voice." To which Bluth adds, "He's got this Santa Claus voice. It isn't the voice of a guy who ever really worries about anything. It's one that gives you a feeling of confidence. He makes you happy. But like a great comedian, behind his mask is a sober man who has seen a lot of life's sadness. And probably that's what keeps the laughs going."

Directing animator Troy Saliba, who was in charge of animating Vlad, adds that although he is a little more cartoonish than most of the film's characters, he is far from "the classic Tex Avery chubby man, with a big head and short legs. He's just a tall man that gained weight over time." Still, his features are fairly simple, as Saliba points out: "his head is basically a salt-and-pepper shaker with a beard, and he has a simplified bean shape for his body."

The lovable Vladimir takes up a lot of room onscreen thanks to both his girth and his grandiose gestures.

Nightmare at Sea

Anya's second confrontation with Rasputin occurs at sea, on the last leg of her journey to Paris. This time, Rasputin has "something more enticing, something really cruel" in mind, as he wishes to lure her to her death through a dream of her imperial past. In so doing, Rasputin seems to call forth the forces of nature as Anya sleepwalks from her cabin to the ship's deck.

The staging of this sequence, like that of the train wreck, is a technical tour de force in which the realism of the computer-generated, three-dimensional settings provides a sharp contrast to

The boat is modeled after a cruise liner that actually existed and belonged to a cousin of Tsar Nicholas.

the seductive dream images.

Anya's dream begins with butterflies circling her face as a vision of Alexei, her younger brother, appears to her in a meadow and she starts to go after him. These serene images are intercut with scenes of Anya sleepwalking as the boat pitches violently in the storm. As Alexei leaps into a pool where her father, Tsar Nicholas, and sisters are swimming, Anya reaches the railing on deck, "inching toward death," and Dimitri tries to reach her. Washed up into the crow's nest by the storm's waves, he seizes a rope, swings over, and grabs her just as her

vision of her father turns into Rasputin.

"Early on," Phil Cruden, head of the layout department, recalls, "it was proposed that the model for the boat be the *Standart*, the Romanov family yacht. But it was soon decided that it should be something larger, but still something she could recognize; this turned out to be the *Tasha*, which Kaiser Wilhelm, the tsar's cousin, had converted into a cruise liner from a battleship. We eventually found a model of the original boat, but from when it was a battleship. So we had to take all the gunnery off and add the railings before we could use it. James Bluth, Don's brother, actually put it together and did a great job on it."

It was from layout drawings based on this model that the final three-dimensional boat was created. In addition, all the ship's cabins were also created digitally, allowing the shots on the boat to be given an appropriate rocking motion. This was considerably more sophisticated than what directing animator Troy Saliba calls "the old-fashioned way, where they would just draw a room against which to animate the characters, leaving it to the camera to make the side-to-side motions.

"The way we did it in *Anastasia*," Saliba says, "looks much nicer, but it was much harder for us [to animate against a moving background]." Chris Shouten, character designer and key character layout artist, concurs, pointing out that "you have to move the character with every single frame of the boat tilting or turning. You simply can't cut any corners."

The animators were at times helped by the provision of digital guides. For instance, Shouten describes the shots where "Anya is standing on the edge at the ship's railing and the camera swings all the

way around to the other side of the boat. That had to be totally mapped and built in the computer first, and then we put our character on it. The challenge here is animating the character in the same dimension, but the computer artists helped by putting in a little wire-frame representation of Anya, to show how big she was and how she was changing perspective. Otherwise, you'd be trying to eyeball the whole thing all the time. I don't think the marrying of the animation with the three-dimensional backgrounds would have been as successful as it is."

A shaken Anya is awoken from a sleepwalking dream-turned-nightmare in the nick of time.

This color key shows Rasputin sending Anya into a nightmare to lure her to a death at sea.

Chapter Four

Paris

❧

Following the tumultuous journey by train and boat, the story changes pace as the action shifts to Paris. The mood becomes less melodramatic and at once more festive and more poignant. ☞ In her Paris home, the Dowager Empress Marie is seeing yet another young woman trying to pass herself off as Anastasia. Broken-hearted, Marie tells Sophie, "No, my heart can't take it anymore! I will see no more girls claiming to be Anastasia," and she symbolically places the photo of Anastasia on her desk facedown. ☞ Soon after, Anya, Dimitri, and Vladimir arrive at Sophie's house. Vladimir and Sophie have a joyous reunion as they mutter affectionately to one another—he gushes, "Sophie Stanislovskievna Somorkov-Smirnoff," while she squeals back, "Vladimir Vanya Voinitsky Vasilovich." It is clear that Vladimir is once again in his element and, in a very real sense, is home again. ☞ Despite Marie's injunction, Sophie questions Anya and ends by asking, "How did you escape from the siege of the palace?" Dimitri and Vladimir are surprised by the question, but when Anya answers, "There was a boy, a boy who worked in the palace. He opened a wall," Dimitri immediately knows that Anya *is* Anastasia. Stunned, he ignores the fact that Anya has passed the test and unconsciously wanders outside unnoticed. ☞ Dimitri must now face up to the unexpected reality of the situation and of his own past, including his part in saving Anastasia and Marie when he was a boy, and the fact that he has fallen in love with the Grand Duchess Anastasia Nicholaievna, heir to the Russian throne. Meanwhile, Vladimir, acting very much like Professor Henry Higgins, says to Anya, "You hear that, child. . . . You did it!" ☞ Their ardor, though, is cooled when Sophie informs them that Marie will not see them. After Vladimir pleads with her, Sophie mentions that the Russian ballet is "performing in Paris tonight [and] we *never* miss

Left: Conceptual art for the Impressionist-style art used frequently in the Paris sequences.

it." Sophie offers to take everybody shopping, leading to the bright "Paris Holds the Key to Your Heart" number. This sequence, Don Bluth notes, shows "Paris brimming with life, while in Russia everything was dying." But amid all this joy, Dimitri also sings, "Paris holds the key to your past. Yes, Princess, I've found you at last. No more pretend. You'll be gone. That's the end." ✒ That night, on the steps of the Paris opera house Dimitri is finally able to convince Vladimir that Anya is the real Anastasia. Dimitri adds that he "will walk out of her life forever," but first, "We're going to go through with this as if nothing has changed." Vladimir urges Dimitri to tell Anya what he knows, but all he can tell her is "How beautiful you look." ✒ In the theater, despite Sophie's attempts to help, Dimitri is unable to get Marie to see Anya. Marie finally has Dimitri removed from her private box, after realizing he is "that con man from St. Petersburg, who was holding auditions to find an Anastasia look-alike," adding, "How much pain will you

inflict on an old woman for money?!" ◄ Overhearing the conversation, Anya is furious at Dimitri for having lied to her and runs away, not wanting to hear what he has to say. Frustrated by this turn of events, Dimitri kidnaps Marie by slipping into her limousine and driving off with her to Sophie's house. There, he finally convinces Marie to see Anya, after showing her the music box. ◄ Marie comes upon Anya unannounced, just as she is packing to leave Paris. After a brief encounter, Marie starts to leave, saying, "I've had enough." Anya, though, recognizes the scent of the peppermint oil Marie uses and remembers when she spilled a bottle of it as a child. Then Marie recognizes the key around Anya's neck and pulls out the music box, tearfully saying, "It was our secret. My Anastasia's and mine." Anya, remembering how it works, puts the key in the box, and they both sing the lullaby, "Hear this song and remember. Soon you'll be home with me, once upon a December," as they embrace. ◄

Paris in the 1920s

In the 1920s, Paris had an almost mystical appeal that attracted artists, writers, musicians, dancers, and entertainers from all over the world. It was the city that welcomed the wholesome American aviator Charles Lindbergh and his plane, *The Spirit of St. Louis*, at the end of his flight across the Atlantic. It also welcomed a host of lesser-known Americans, including aspiring composers like Aaron Copland and Virgil Thomson, who came to study composition with Nadia Boulanger, while Ernest Hemingway, F. Scott Fitzgerald, and Gertrude Stein came to write.

For African Americans, Paris was a place to escape the bigotry back home. American jazz became all the rage, and entertainers like Bricktop and the fabulous Josephine Baker wowed the crowds while Langston Hughes and other writers of the Harlem Renaissance joined the rest of America's Lost Generation.

Artists Pablo Picasso, Joan Miró, and Salvador Dalí emigrated from Spain, along with Tsuguharu Foujita from Japan and Giorgio de Chirico from Italy. In 1922 Ireland's James Joyce published his groundbreaking novel *Ulysses* for the first time in Paris.

Paris in the 1920s was also a place of refuge, becoming home to a vibrant colony of Russian émigrés, many of them aristocrats fleeing the revolution and its aftermath.

One of the key figures in this mix was Sergei Diaghilev,

whose Ballets Russes (Russian Ballet) commissioned music from some of Europe's leading composers. These included Igor Stravinsky, who wrote such groundbreaking ballets as *The Firebird* and *The Rite of Spring*, as well as French composers Maurice Ravel (*Daphnis and Chloé*) and Claude Debussy (*Jeux*). He also hired such avant-garde artists as French cubist painter Georges Braque to design sets and costumes.

The Ballets Russes included in its company such major dancers and choreographers as Fokine, Nijinsky, and Léonide Massine, who were joined in

1924 by the young George Balanchine, having just defected from a touring Soviet company.

Other Russian émigrés included pioneer puppet animator Ladislas Starevich, whose career flourished in France, as did that of Russian film star Ivan Mozhukhin, whose credits include a celebrated version of *Casanova*, and artists Marc Chagall and Alexander Archipenko.

The French were far from inactive in their own capital. Although Paris took the American flapper to its heart, it was still the home of *haute couture* and the scandalous

designs of Coco Chanel. It nurtured the careers of entertainers Maurice Chevalier and Mistinguete and hosted the Folies Bergère. The 1920s also saw the birth of modern French cinema, when such noted directors as Jean Renoir and René Clair got their start, and Abel Gance created *Napoleon*, the world's first widescreen epic. French writer André Breton started the surrealist movement, based largely on the writings and teachings of Viennese psychologist Sigmund Freud. One of the most famous surrealist works of the period was the film *An Andalusian Dog*, in which the

Spaniard Luis Buñuel made his directing debut with Salvador Dalí.

Local artists included Marcel Duchamp, the creator of dadaism; Fernand Léger; and Francis Picabia. In 1925, the Exposition des Arts Décoratifs et Industriels sparked the art deco movement, just as the Exposition Universelle, held in Paris in 1900, had launched art nouveau. French composers Darius Milhaud and Erik Satie were contemporaries of Debussy and Ravel, while literary lights included André Gide and Jean Cocteau, who went on to do a bit of filmmaking as well.

Left: A daytime inspiration sketch along the Seine River. Below: Paris is drawn quite differently than St. Petersburg. For instance, the sketches of Paris are much more romantic and include curved lines and winding roads.

View from the Seine overlooking the Louvre.

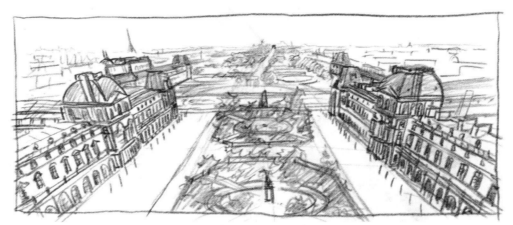

The Louvre courtyard.

The rear entrance to the Louvre.

Along the Seine.

The main entrance to the courtyard of the Louvre.

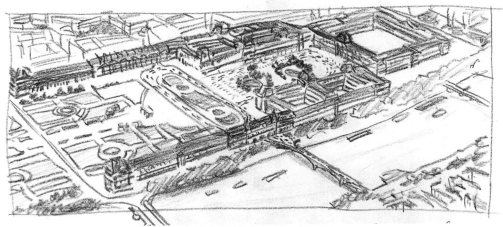

An aerial shot of the Louvre and the Seine.

A second angle on the Louvre courtyard.

The front of the Louvre across from the Seine.

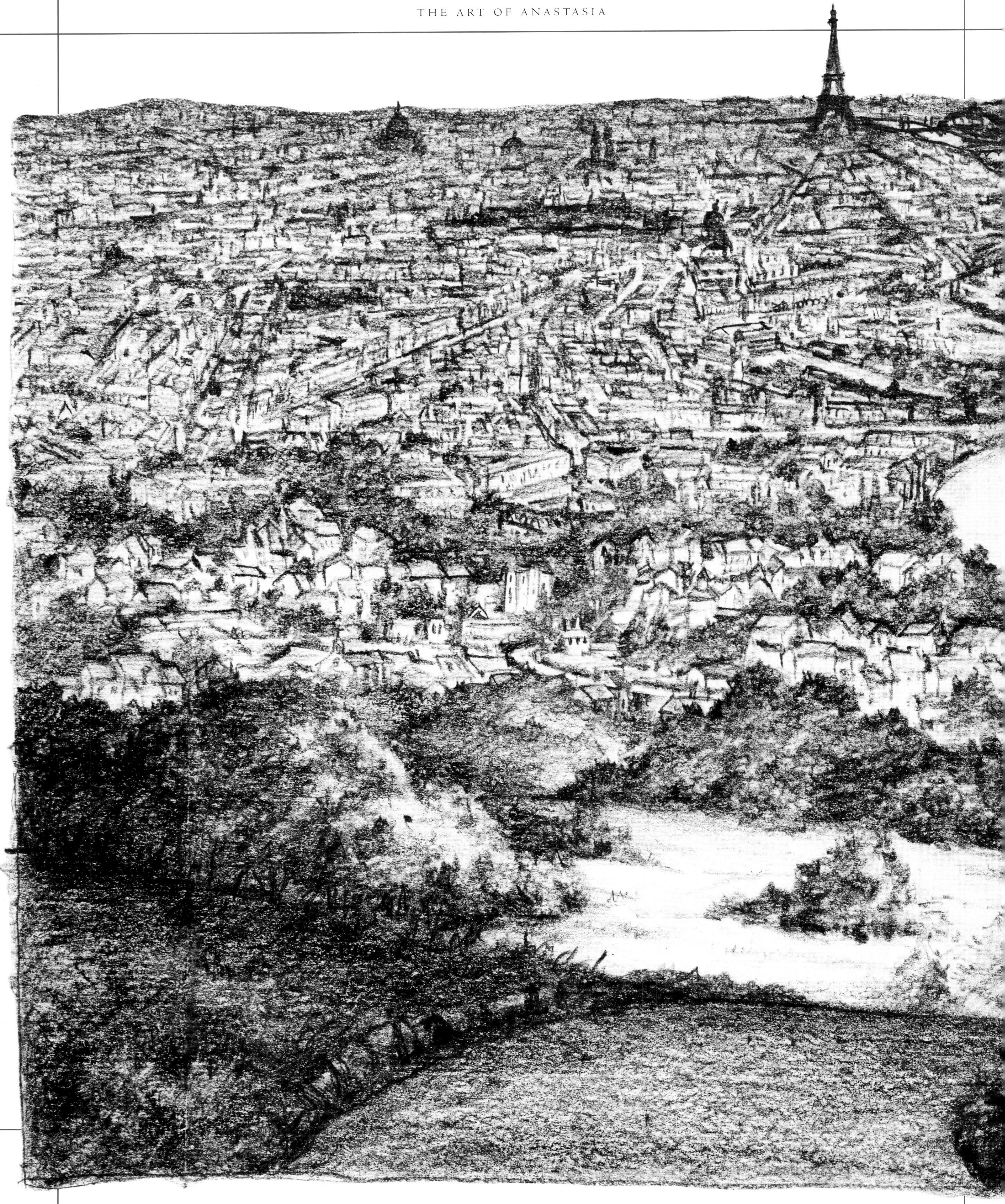

Above: Background art for a late evening on the street where Sophie lives.

Bottom, from left to right: Two inspirational sketches from "Paris Holds the Key" and a rough layout for the above image.

Sophie's Choice. *Sophie is at first reluctant to speak with Anya due to all of the false Anastasias she has seen before (above). However, Anya's answers surprise everyone, most of all Dimitri, who realizes that Anya is the real thing.*

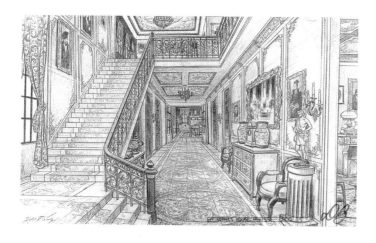

*Line drawings of Sophie's
Paris apartment include two
views of the entrance hall and
living room as well as a
rough layout of the exterior.*

Paris Holds the Key to Your Heart

"Paris Holds the Key to Your Heart" is a dazzling showstopper conceived by Lynn Ahrens and Stephen Flaherty. It not only pays homage to Paris in the 1920s but also salutes the Hollywood cartoons of the 1930s and the classic rapid-fire montage sequences of Slavko Vorkapich. Of course, in their animated film, Don Bluth and Gary Goldman were able to add a few tricks of their own.

"We needed to get the feeling," Bluth says, "that Paris was the hub of international society in the 1920s. Fashion and hairstyles were changing. Lindbergh was landing his airplane, Mickey Mouse in *Steamboat Willie* opened in Paris, and Maurice Chevalier was on the stage of the Moulin Rouge. American artists migrated to Paris to study. Celebrities congregated there. In other words, Paris was changing and brimming with life, while in Russia everything was dying.

"It was a wonderful time, and I don't think we've even touched on what a marvelous, enlightened period it was. But we thought, 'Well, maybe we can just mention a few names,' so that you get an idea of the change from Russia."

Thus, as Sophie belts out her welcome to Paris, we are treated, in the manner of old cartoons that put celebrities on parade, to cameo appearances by Maurice Chevalier, Sigmund Freud, Charles Lindbergh (in his plane, of course), Josephine Baker, Claude Monet, Auguste Rodin (which is a bit of a stretch, since he died in 1917), and Gertrude Stein. In addition, Anya gets one of her dresses at—where else?—Coco Chanel's.

Goldman admits, "Most young people under twenty-five will not know who all these people are, but it should be fun for some of the older people in the audience."

The contrast between Paris and St. Petersburg is heightened by the fact that the characters are seen inside paintings by Monet and other French artists. On a more subtle level, the cities were drawn differently. Paris is softer, with the emphasis on art nouveau styling. However, when the characters go shopping, there is also quite a bit of the newer art deco and Impressionist/Pointillist backgrounds added as well.

All this joy and exuberance, however, does little to cheer up Dimitri, who knows he is losing Anya.

Paris Holds the Key. *After Sophie generously offers to take Anya and her friends shopping, Anya finds that Paris does indeed hold the key to her heart.*

The Ballet. *Anya, Dimitri, and Vladimir attend the ballet. Above, top to bottom: Anastasia's transformation is complete. Once inside the opera house, Dimitri attempts to calm Anya while he plans her introduction to Marie. Sophie and Dimitri approach Marie, who is already seated in her box.*

Top: The production background of Marie's suite at the Paris opera house. Bottom, from left to right: A conceptual painting for the opera house stage set; an early conceptual design for the Sleeping Beauty *stage set; and the set design of the interior of the main entrance of the opera house—inspired by the Opéra de Paris.*

A Confrontation. *"You're that con man."* *Disbelieving of Dimitri's intentions, Marie refuses to speak with him. Ignoring Sophie's signals to leave, Dimitri is forcibly removed from the box. His attempts to console Anya only make matters worse.*

149

Kidnapped! *In an effort to convince Marie that he has found the lost Princess Anastasia, Dimitri commandeers her car, then surprises her with something she thought lost long ago—Anastasia's music box.*

The guest bedroom that Anastasia
occupies shares the warm coloring that
typifies the color scheme used for Paris.
The frames on the walls remain empty
until the separately painted portraits
are "hung," using computer technology.

  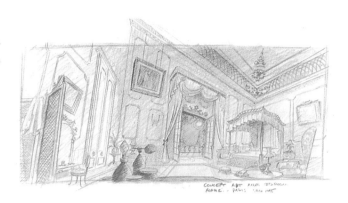

Since the real Marie never lived in Paris, the team at Fox had to rely on imagination supported by period pieces and architectural details to reflect

her wealth and the time in which she lived. Although some of the earlier concept sketches feature a more prominent bed, the bed that was

settled on derives from a real Romanov possession captured in photographs by the Romanov family themselves in Russia.

History Meets Fantasy: Marie's Bedroom

Although many of the details and visual elements of *Anastasia* are authentic, including Anya's bedroom in Russia, Marie's lavish Paris apartment is "pure fantasy." Don Bluth says, "Marie actually moved to Denmark once the revolution got underway, after the family's demise. We put her in a more romantic location, one that everyone would recognize: Paris. We know she was very rich, so we needed an extravagant environment which would reflect what this woman represents: wealth, money, royalty, aristocracy, the blue blood." The apartment is a period set with well-researched props and architectural details, but, unlike the other settings in the movie, which are historically accurate, this grandiose room is a child of pure imagination.

Although the look of the apartment reflects Marie and her wealth, the tone of the scene, like that of every other in the film, is established by its color scheme. "This is a closure moment in the picture," Bluth explains. "In this scene Anya finally puts the tragedy of her past to rest as she looks at photographs of her family and remembers them. It's a happy moment." Many possible colors were considered for the scene; green was rejected as too peaceful and blue as too passive. "The emotional target," Bluth says, "is satisfaction, fulfillment, and resolution. The scene requires warm, loving colors: ambers, burgundies, pinks, et cetera."

In addition to the color scheme for the scene, layout artist Daniel Chiang needed to design the room so that it fit the requirements of layout department head Phil Cruden: "palacelike, French, and feminine." Just as important was that Chiang leave "some acting space," avoiding any clutter that could "distract from the animation." For instance, notice the open space between the chairs and couch and the mirror on the right, where Marie places the crown on Anya's head.

Left: A production background for the back waiting room in the Grand Palais.

Bottom: the color key for Marie's bedroom.

The Reunion. *"I know very well who you thought I was. Who exactly are you?" With the help of the smell of peppermint, the music box, and her necklace, Anastasia and her grandmother are reunited at last.*

Another Memory Returns. *As the music box plays its haunting melody, the lyrics to her special lullaby come rushing back to Anastasia.*

Marie and Sophie

For Don Bluth, the character of the Dowager Empress Marie "was the easiest one of all to develop." However, Gary Goldman adds, "What wasn't easy was the real woman. When you really look into her background, she was generally a terrible person. So, we created a grandmother that was going to be more appealing to most people."

"I just ignored the real woman," Bluth says. "Once we had Angela Lansbury and got her voice, then it was easy to draw the character. At that point, it was also pretty easy to write the lines, because she has a different personality.

"Helen Hayes played the grandmother [in the Ingrid Bergman version] as an understanding woman, although she was fiercely stubborn and principled; that Marie was so protected by a shell she put around herself, because she didn't want to be hurt anymore. Our Marie is a little softer and not quite as encased in a hard shell; she is a *little* more open and less closed up."

In many ways, Marie is the most subtly designed of all the characters. As Troy Saliba, the directing animator responsible for her, says, "She was enjoyable to work on because

of her elegance and refinement. I took the design that Don was working on, got some angles happening on the facial structure, which I really enjoyed drawing from different perspectives. Her crown, though, was a bit of a chore, but she was on the opposite side of the scale from Vlad," the other character Saliba was in charge of.

For directing animator Paul Newberry, Marie was his "favorite character to do, perhaps because of what Angela Lansbury was doing. She was really good, and the actress they cast to do the live-action [reference footage] was also very good.

"What was most difficult," he adds, "was the line work and the precision needed in drawing her, as she's one of the slowest-moving characters in the film. You really have to control the volumes and shapes. I really didn't find it hard, because it's something that I get pleasure from when it's working well. Her movements are very subtle and contrast sharply with Sophie, who is very bubbly and always jumping all over the place."

"When we got the idea for Sophie," Bluth says, "we knew that she was part of that great

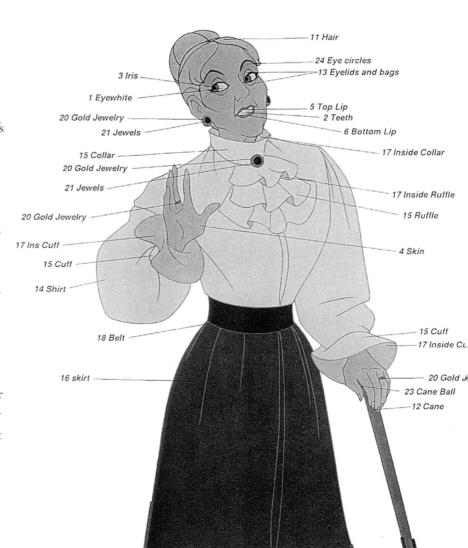

aristocracy that went to live in Paris because of the revolution. She is also the confidante of her cousin Marie, the one who Marie expresses all of her feelings to. That's her purpose in the play.

"Sophie really doesn't make too many major plot suggestions herself; she mainly reacts off the other characters. Also, since she and Vladimir were probably very romantic with each other at one time, it gives him a way to get back into the aristocracy. Sophie is not really a main, main character; rather, she is one of the clowns that helps keep the levity going.

"Bernadette Peters," he adds, "was probably the first suggestion for Sophie's voice, and the one we just went for and got. Bernadette is petite and has a lot of cute mannerisms, but we decided not to fashion Sophie after her; instead, we wanted her to be very much the mirror image of Vladimir, so she's a lot more corpulent.

"I remember, in the very beginning, one of the writers saying, 'It's two little chubby hands reaching for the same Danish pastry.' And that image always stuck in my mind."

Keep the Money. *"It was more of a change of heart."* Dimitri
surprises Marie by refusing the reward money and chooses not to share
this information with Anastasia.

Music and Song

The songwriting team of Lynn Ahrens (lyrics) and Stephen Flaherty (music) clearly play a vital role in shaping *Anastasia*. As Kevin Bannerman, vice president of production, Fox Family Films, notes, "the songwriters always are the ones who spot the songs. And in doing that, they help define when you're going to learn what about the characters."

Robert Kraft, executive vice president of music, Fox Filmed Entertainment, recalls that before Ahrens and Flaherty were hired, they were asked to write two demo songs. "I remember very distinctly," he says, "hearing them in a room in Phoenix with Don, Gary, Bill Mechanic, and several others. One of the songs in particular, 'Once Upon a December,' got everyone excited, and ended up being one of the great songs of the film."

The fact that a music box was a focal point of *Anastasia* intrigued Ahrens and Flaherty because, as Ahrens points out, "it was a musical motif built right into the movie." They felt that the scene where Anya walks into the old palace and has an intense sense of déjà vu could be an incredible animated sequence, where, in Ahrens's words, "here the memories, inspired by this melody she remembers from her past, begin to come to life." "These memories also," as Flaherty notes, "musically burst into the large choral sound of Russia, representing all of the people that had been part of the Romanov era."

The song, "Once Upon a December," was also used in the prologue and in the reunion scene late in the film and became one of the film's principal motifs used in the musical underscore written by David Newman. (Newman, incidentally, is the son of film music pioneer Alfred Newman, who wrote the score for the earlier 1956 Fox version of *Anastasia*.)

The other song the duo wrote for their audition was "Rumor in St. Petersburg," which was also their first attempt at an opening number. "Somehow or another," Ahrens notes, "it was pushed aside. At one point, people thought we should musicalize the entire prologue. So we wrote the Russian Revolution, in music and song, in three minutes. It was fabulous, but it didn't end up in the movie. Then there was a piece of that called 'The Rulers of Russia,' a glorious sort of a waltz piece, which introduced the Romanov family. Then, [Kevin Bannerman] said, 'What about that "Rumor in St. Petersburg" number?' We revisited and revised it, and simplified it a bit, and that's what ended up in the movie."

The song has a certain earthy quality to it, with perhaps the most pronounced Russian quality of all the musical numbers. Flaherty admits, "Prokofiev and Tchaikovsky were big influences, and I was also listening to a lot of Russian peasant music, whose rhythms are so contagious." The klezmer scales and harmonies he was using for *Ragtime*, which he was writing at the same time, may have also found their way into the song.

Ahrens says, "What we try very hard to do as songwriters is to build visuals in. We always try to write a song that has action involved in it, whether it's for the stage or screen; we make sure that it can be dramatized in some way and doesn't require a character to just stand there and sing, because it's going to be boring." And indeed, the song quickly introduces St. Petersburg and two of the main characters and their scheme, all in a few minutes.

The next two songs, Anya's "Journey to the Past" and Rasputin's "In the Dark of the Night," were the two hardest for Ahrens and Flaherty to write. They are both classic music moments, the "I am" or "I want" songs, which define who a character is. The two tried a number of different approaches to Anya's song before ending up with "Journey to the Past." Their breakthrough, Flaherty says, came after Carrie Fisher wrote a new scene where Anya literally comes to a crossroads and tries to decide which way to go for her future.

"At the beginning," he says, "I provided a little musical vamp (a musical figure that becomes the basis of the accompaniment) that would start and then stop, start again and then stop. I was trying to illustrate, in the accompaniment, her hesitancy about what choice to make. And that was the jumping off point for the song. I also had the voice of Liz Callaway [Anya's singing voice] implanted in my ear. Because I knew Liz's big note, I knew it would have to end on that note, and that it could start with this start and stop vamp. And from that, I basically wrote towards the middle."

The problem with Rasputin's song, "In the Dark of the Night," was trying to find out who exactly this villain was; after exploring different directions, the song, in Ahrens's words, "gelled down to what we have now: that he is a powerful, somewhat funny, but mostly terrifying villain, who is out for revenge, and who is funny without knowing he's funny."

Flaherty adds, "Robert Kraft suggested more of a rock sound for Rasputin, seeing him almost as a rock star, with this sort of mane of wild hair.

So, it ended up having more of a rock underpinning and less rooted to the realistic world of Russia in the twenties. We figured that limbo was a place where anything could happen, including rock music!" Eventually, Meat Loaf producer Jim Steinman came in to rearrange Ahrens's and Flaherty's song.

The "Learn to Do It" number, in which Vladimir starts preparing Anya for her meeting with the Dowager Empress, incidentally reveals facts about Anya's past. Once again, as Ahrens puts it, "there's a dramatic function to the song. It takes her not only on a journey from urchin to princess, but from Russia to France. There's a lot of action involved and it's a bit of a tongue twister, but it's a lot of fun."

Ahrens's and Flaherty's initial inspiration for this number was "Tchaikovsky," the song that Danny Kaye made famous in the Kurt Weill–Ira Gershwin musical, *Lady in the Dark*, by rattling off the names of Russian composers in quick succession. Indeed, the first incarnation of "Learn to Do It" had Vladimir rattling off all the names of Anastasia's Russian relatives.

"It was Bill Mechanic," Flaherty said, "who felt the number should have more active comedy, and be more about teaching Anya how to walk or gesture. So, we balanced the

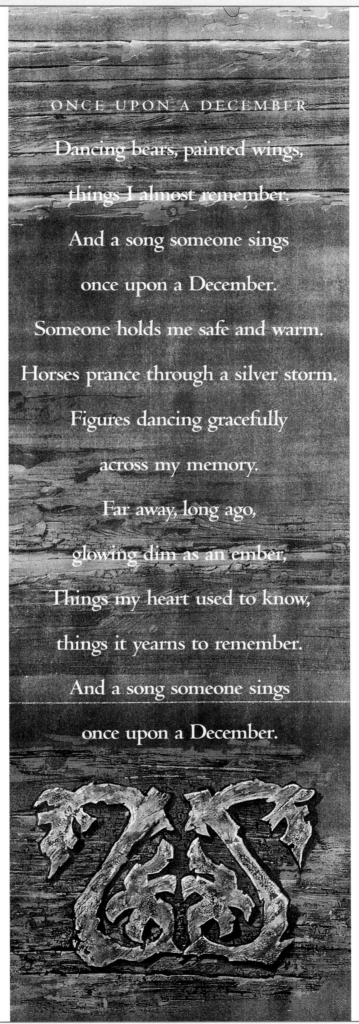

ONCE UPON A DECEMBER

Dancing bears, painted wings,

things I almost remember.

And a song someone sings

once upon a December.

Someone holds me safe and warm.

Horses prance through a silver storm.

Figures dancing gracefully

across my memory.

Far away, long ago,

glowing dim as an ember,

Things my heart used to know,

things it yearns to remember.

And a song someone sings

once upon a December.

wordplay, the facts, and the physical comedy."

The next number, "The Learn to Do It Reprise" is another teaching song (Anya is learning to waltz) but this one is done in waltz time. Flaherty says, "We wanted this to be a reprise moment for Vladimir, where he sees the two youngsters falling in love, and it's almost like, 'Oh, my God, what have I done?' sort of emotion. We also wanted to point out musically that Vladimir, although he is a comic guy, is actually a very romantic and poetic character. The song enabled us to give him that moment and, at the same time, focus on the fact that Anya and Dimitri were indeed falling in love."

The last production number, "Paris Holds the Key," turned out to be the easiest to write. Flaherty comments, "The final look of the sequence, with its use of French Impressionist paintings, which seems a nod to MGM's *American in Paris*, with Gene Kelly going through Paris in the style of Toulouse-Lautrec, is Don Bluth's." Ahrens continues, "It is both a great big, fun production number, taking in Paris of the twenties, and it centerpieces Dimitri, who is having a terrible time, because he realizes he's fallen in love with Anya and won't be able to have her after all."

Chapter Five

Coda

Rasputin, who has made a clock tower his Parisian hideout, plans to kill Anastasia at her coronation party and "crush her at the height of her glory."

Bartok, tired of all these shenanigans, tells him to "Forget the girl, and get a life." "Oh," Rasputin replies, "I'll get a life, Bartok. Hers!" ➤ Meanwhile, at Marie's, she and Anya have what Bluth calls one of the film's "Cinderella moments. The grandmother leads Anya, who is wearing these cute little pajamas, over to the mirror and says, 'You have the beauty of your mother.' Marie then opens a box and takes out *the* crown and puts it on Anya's head. Then we do a match dissolve, and suddenly it's not just a crown, it's the whole dress she's wearing. It is then that she becomes a new person; not just any girl, but a member of the royal family." ➤ Later, when Marie offers Dimitri his reward, he refuses to take the money. She asks him, "You were ... the servant boy who got us out? You saved her life, and mine. Then you restored her to me, yet you want no reward." He tells her his decision "was more a change of heart." He says good-bye to Vladimir before going back to St.

Left: A color key of the Grand Palais during the Inaugural Ball celebrating the return of the princess Anastasia.

Petersburg, telling him, "Trust me, this is the one thing I'm doing right." ⟶ With the party at the Louvre in full swing, Marie comes upon Anya, who is waiting to be presented to the guests but nevertheless seems unhappy. Marie tells Anya, "He didn't take the money," which both surprises and confuses Anya. She is then left alone to decide what to do. Pooka runs barking out the door and Anastasia follows him into the Tuileries garden. The garden magically closes in around her, forcing her in a single direction.

Anya tries to flee across the bridge, where she encounters Rasputin. ⟶ "The final confrontation," Bluth notes, "was very difficult. Rasputin holds all the cards. He's got a magic wand, if you will, in the reliquary, in which he has all the power he needs to kill this girl. But the silly man elects, rather than just killing her, to toy with her and enjoy the moment, which is his downfall. Because in so doing, she manages to wrestle it out of his hand and smash it. She doesn't know she is actually destroying him when she destroys it.

She only knows that that reliquary is what empowers him. So she tries to get rid of it. "Also, when Anastasia confronts him, the last pieces of her memory fall into place, and she now remembers him and what he did. This is the creature that robbed her of that wonderful childhood, robbed her of her family, robbed her of everything. And it's her own private demon that she has to fight. And neither Dimitri nor anybody else can come in and save her." Bluth also explains, "We had a really tough time boarding it, because if you bring Dimitri back into it, which I think you have to, it's very easy to just have a 'boy rescues girl' situation. We had many versions where he would come back in and he became the strong one. In the end, we didn't let him rescue her. Rasputin keeps him busy, so Dimitri isn't really able to assist her. She has to do it herself." With Rasputin out of the way, Dimitri and Anya are finally able to admit their love for each other and start a new life together.

Seeing that Pooka does not look very comfortable in his new finery, Vladimir relieves him of one of his medals.

Fabergé Eggs

The music box, which Marie gives the young Anastasia in the prologue, was a central part of the film from the very beginning; in fact, the movie's working title was *The Music Box*. The music box itself is fashioned in the style of a Fabergé egg, the most illustrious product of the fabled House of Fabergé in St. Petersburg.

Originally founded by jeweler Gustav Fabergé, its rise to fame occurred under the leadership of his son, Peter Carl Fabergé, who took over the business with his brother Agathon in 1870. Carl expanded the business to include the manufacture of decorative objects, and when the products of his workshops were showcased at the Pan-Russian Exhibition in Moscow in 1882, the company began to enjoy the patronage of the imperial family, along with that of other European royal houses.

Easter is Russia's most important religious holiday and was traditionally celebrated by the exchange of decorated eggs, representing both new life and resurrection. In 1885 Alexander III gave a Fabergé egg to his wife, the Empress Marie. Thereafter, it became an Easter tradition in the Romanov family. Nicholas II

not only gave Fabergé eggs to his wife at Easter but also gave them to his mother, the Dowager Empress.

The first imperial egg was rather simple in design. Made of gold, with white enameling on the outside to resemble a chicken egg, it opened to reveal a surprise in the form of a golden hen with ruby eyes, along with a ruby egg hanging from a miniature imperial crown. Subsequent eggs were more elaborate, both inside and out, and were made of other precious metals and gems, including diamonds.

For instance, in 1909 Nicholas gave Alexandra an egg that contained a tiny, detailed replica of the imperial yacht, the *Standart*. Some contained moving parts or even clocks, as was the case with the cuckoo-clock egg given to Alexandra in 1900; when a button at the back of the clock was pressed, a bird emerged and started cuckooing, while moving its beak and wings. Other eggs contained such mechanical elements as a revolving display of miniature paintings or an elephant that walked with a swaying motion, its head and tail moving back and forth.

To celebrate the 300th anniversary of Romanov rule,

Nicholas presented Alexandra with an egg decorated on the outside with gold double-headed eagles and crowns, along with miniature paintings of eighteen Romanov rulers; the egg contained a blue steel globe, with one half showing the Russian empire in 1613, and the other showing it in 1913.

Although the design of the film's music box egg was original, it is not without its precedents. In 1904 Nicholas presented Alexandra with an egg featuring a replica of Uspensky Cathedral in Moscow, where he was crowned in

1896. It also contained a music box, wound by a gold key, that played a hymn.

The last Fabergé egg known to be made for the imperial family was delivered in 1916. The House of Fabergé, which closed its Moscow and London branches during World War I, was taken over by a People's Committee in 1917; because the new Soviet government had no use for the elaborate baubles the company made, it was closed in 1918. Peter Carl Fabergé escaped to Switzerland, where he died in 1920.

In order to create the perfect music box, various sketches were

done of actual Fabergé eggs and several period music boxes.

Above: This final design was given to the 3-D crew as a model.

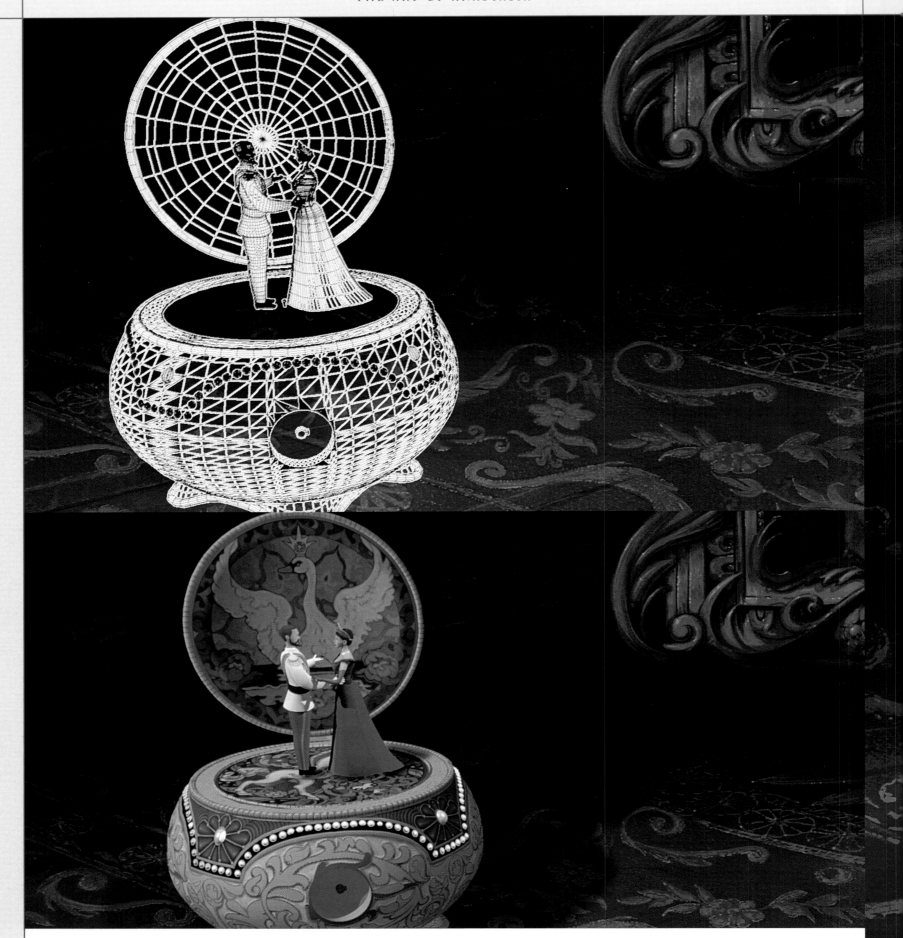

In order to bring the music box to life, the 3-D department built it into their computer.

Here we see three stages of its production: wireframe (top), texture mapping (bottom), and final (right).

Into Harm's Way. *Anastasia leaves the ball to retrieve a fleeing Pooka. Guided by his barks she quickly becomes lost in the garden maze and senses danger. Rasputin emerges and enlists his minions to help him get rid of Anastasia once and for all.*

To the Rescue. *The bridge crumbles under Anastasia's feet and she dangles from the edge at Rasputin's mercy. Both Pooka and Dimitri run to her aid, but their efforts only put them in danger. It is up to Anastasia to save them all.*

Happily Ever After

In one sense, a film's ending should be simple. As Bluth says, "The wrapping of the movie, after the fight, is just a matter of Dimitri and Anya finally admitting that they are more than passing strangers; that they really mean something to each other and are finally able to articulate that. And there you have the happy ending."

However, it is not as easy as it seems, because Anya also has to decide between her new-found life with her grandmother and her future with Dimitri. The latter scenes involving Anya, Marie, and Dimitri are the reason that Bluth and Goldman were initially wary of adapting the story for animation.

As Kevin Bannerman points out, "The whole last section in the Ingrid Bergman movie is very elliptical, because people are not saying what they mean; what they mean is all subtext. But what they're saying, they're saying because they think it's what they have to say. It's all about not saying what you feel.

"Well, you can't do that in animation. You have to be clearer. One of the struggles we had in the screenplay was these very emotional scenes. Our challenge was to say things clearly and yet subtly, leaving no doubt as to what was happening." It wasn't until after the film was previewed that the final changes to the ending were made, which clarified the relationship between Marie and Anya.

"*Anastasia*," Bluth says, "is what I call a purpose abandonment story. Anya sets out to find her family, which drives her through most of the movie. But when she finds out Dimitri didn't take the money, she realizes that maybe her home isn't just living with Grandma. Her real home and happiness and future lie with this young

man, who brought her back to her grandmother. At first he did it for selfish reasons, but he was then willing to walk away because he knew that princesses don't marry kitchen boys.

"To make the happy ending really work, you say, 'Yes, she was willing to give up the title and go away with Dimitri, but would she ever lose Grandmama?'

"At the same time, Marie realizes, 'I can either cling to her, or I can let her go.' In the end, she lets Anya go in a very dignified way, saying, 'I wonder if you really want this? There might be something else that is happiness for you, that is your world.' Then the grandmother adds, 'He didn't take the money,' and then, 'But whatever you decide, we will always have each other.' Which means they won't lose each other. So, Anya doesn't lose Grandma. What she gives up is her title."

"Hopefully there are many things that people will walk away with after seeing this movie," Donley notes. "We tried to provide a context that would play out the timeless and universal truths of parents' everlasting love for their children and the need for those children to eventually strike out on their own. Because, after all, home is not a place but rather the people you love."

"What we're trying to imply," Bluth concludes, "is that Marie's world is something Anastasia once belonged to. At the beginning of the movie she sang 'Journey to the Past,' but the lesson here is that you really can't go back to your past. Yes, you can go back and look at your scrapbook and everything, but it's not relevant." It is with this wisdom that Anastasia is ultimately able to fully integrate her past and build her own future.

Thank you to the following people at Fox Animation Studios for making the movie (and this book!) possible.

Rosie Ahern
Jennifer F. Alton
Jane M. Anderson
Winston B. Aquino
Donato D. Arado
Sarah J. Arado
Jocelyn S. Atienza
Leslie T. Aust
Cesar Avalos
Jason L. Ayon
Kelly Baigent
Adam T. Beck
Victorina C. Belleza
Robert L. Bender
Richard C. Bentham
Thomas M. Bernardo
Colby L. Bluth
Don Bluth
James P. Bluth
Carol D. Bocalan
Edwin Bocalan
Nelson A. Bohol
Anna Braga
John R. Brain
Kenneth A. Brain
Joseph G. Busacca
Mary Crescas Busacca
Tracy A. Butenko
Julie A. Byers
Fiona M. Byrne
Arnel T. Cabanela
Shareena Carlson
Joy C. Carmeci
Troylan B. Caro
Kathy M. Carter-Costello
Gerard T. Carty
Michelle A. Cassidy
Jay E. Chapman
Jian C. Chen
Xiao-Xia Cheng
Hung Yuan Chiang
Gregory M. Chin
Ben S. Choi
Kenneth J. Cioe
Vincent F. Clarke
Mary Clarke-Miller
Jocelyn D. Clemente
Giovanni Colombo
Kevin J. Condron
Richard J. Contadino
Eileen Conway
Courtney A. Cook
Gary S. Cooper
Joseph R. Cop
John S. Corsi
John A. Costello
Nancy A. Cox
Phaedra Craig
Alan T. Cranny
Adam J. Cresswell
Philip A. Cruden
Pearse G. Cullinane
Joel C. Cunanan
Martine Cunningham
Steve A. Cunningham
Cary H. Curley
Suzanne B. D'Arcy
Cynthia A. Dankworth-Kelsey
Joseph J. DeAsis
Manuel A. DeGuzman
Alfonso A. DeLeon
Wilfredo B. DeLeon
Abraham DeOcampo
Stephen J. Deane
Narciso S. Dela Rosa
John C. Devlin
Rafael Diaz Canales
Peter A. Donnelly
Renato F. DosAnjos
Burl L. Doty
Matt P. Dougherty
Scott O. Douthitt
Emmet M. Doyle
Catherine A. Dresbach
Steven J. Dunn
Bruce Edwards
Jeffrey T. Edwards
Carol L. Ellis
Christopher J. Elsner
Matthew K. Englehart
Laurie E. Engler
Shannon M. Enriquez
Zoe J. Evamy
Martin A. Fagan
Albert P. Feliciano
Allan R. Fernando
Linda T. Fitzpatrick
Alan S. Fleming
Nicola J. Flynn
Paul P. Fogarty
Brian J. Forsythe
Robert A. Fox
Donal A. Freeney
Regnerito U. Frondozo
Manuel G. Galiana
Bradley Gayo
Shawn J. Gibson
Debbie J. Gold
Cathy J. Goldman
Gary W. Goldman
Kip M. Goldman
Edison Goncalves
Cynthia M. Gosney
Micah R. Gosney
Alexander Goutman
Randall L. Groom
Kurt J. Grubaugh
Vicky L. Hacker
Carrie-Ann Hall
Gary A. Ham
Greg S. Ham
Scott E. Hamilton
Martin G. Hanley
Noirin M. Hanley
Carol Ann M. Hannan
Liam T. Hannan
David J. Hardy
Sean P. Hart
Karl J. Hayes
Heather L. Heichberger
Richard A. Heichberger
Robert S. Henricks
Rory W. Hensley
John W. Hill
Nichole Hill
John D. Hoffman
Mike J. Hogue
Derek G. Holmes
Stephen L. Holt
Sue Houghton
Roisin P. Hunt
Julian C. Hynes
Cash B. Imutan
Jocellie C. Imutan
Julieta M. Indonila
Barry J. Iremonger
Michael P. Isaak
Roberto Islas
Harper K. Jaten
Jennifer A. Jeras
Jennifer M. Jolls
Jack J. Joseph
Mark A. Kauffman
Linda C. Kaul
Dean T. Kawada
Chris L. Kazmier
Neil W. Keaveney
Bernice H. Keegan
Sandra R. Keely
Paul J. Kelly
Paul M. Kelly
Bernie Keogh-Diaz Canales
Jon J. Kerbaugh
Celine Kiernan
Noel P. Keirnan
Adrian P. Kilkenny
Christie C. Klein
William A. Kobylka
Marek C. Kochout
Frances E. Kumashiro
Christopher J. Kurash
Leonardo C. Lagonera
Michael C. Lahay
John J. Lakey
Siobhan M. Larkin
Jon K. Le Mond
Shelly Leigh
Mathew W. Leivian
Howard J. Levenson
Ricardo B. Licas Jr.
Karri L. Lindamood
Faustino Q. Lofamia Jr.
Brett A. Long
Grant C. Lounsbury
Jeff S. Lujan
Juan A. Luna
David J. Lux
Caroline M. Lynch
Stephen J. Lynes
Suzanne L. Lynes
Diarmuid MacAlasdair
Dave E. MacDougall
Jeannette M. Maher
Lisa M. Maher
William C. Makra
Richard G. Manginsay
Joseph C. Manifold
Brien J. Manning
Shirley A. Mapes
Molly A. Mariani
Jeff J. Marshall
Manuelito G. Martin
Peter J. Matheson
Crystal C. Mathews
Ciara T. McCabe
Jennifer A. McCosker
Helen M. McDevitt
Ryan G. McElhinney
Henry D. McGrane
Brenda M. McGuirk
Robert G. McIntosh
Gareth P. McKinney
James C. McLoughlin
Mark G. McLoughlin
Tracey A. Meighan
Rebecca K. Mendoza
Terry L. Merrill
Rob G. Meyers
Burce F. Miles
Thomas M. Miller
Mark E. Misch
Hamilton W. Mitchell
Maria A. Mitchell
Adriano S. Mondala Jr.
Cesar S. Mondala
Kate M. Moo King
Sharon E. Morgan
Fernando Moro
Ciaran F. Morris
John L. Morris Jr.
Katherine M. Morris
Paul A. Morris
Lyn J. Mulvany
David B. Munier
Anne C. Murray-O'Craobhach
Danelle L. Murtaugh
Cynthia A. Nason
Robyn C. Nason
Kelly J. Nelson
Lance M. Nelson
Maximillan V. Nepomuceno
Pete C. Newbauer
Paul A. Newberry
Amy L. Newman
Maire Sorcha Ni Chuimin
Darren P. Nicoll
Derek J. Nielsen
David E. O'Brien
John W. O'Flaherty
Carmen D. Oliver
Debbie Olshan
Cris M. Olson
Raquel V. Omana
Aran O'Reilly
Suzanne O'Reilly
Jespeh G. Orrantia
Terence A. O'Toole
Andee K. Ott
Chip Pace
Slava Pazhitnov
Jose S. Paraiso Jr.
Enrico D. Paz
Slava Pazhitnov
Victoria R. Pena
Shannon S. Penner
Michael B. Pennington
Alejandro M. Perez
Laura M. Gianas Perez
Yuri Petrochenkov
John E. Piegzik
Andrzej J. Piotrowski
Marco O. Plantilla
John P. Power
Tod W. Price
Nick A. Quan
David M. Rabbitte
Angelito B. Ramos
John P. Rand
Pio D. Ravago III
Robert J. Reed
Fred A. Reilly
Rick I. Remender
Deirdre M. Reynolds-Behan
John B. Rice
Frank J. Richards
Michael T. Rider
Olun M. Riley
Alberto M. Rodriguez
Owen J. Rohu
Edward A. Rooney
Eric J. Ryan
Jason G. Salata
Troy D. Saliba
Joven Sampang
David W. Satchwell
Amy Savage
Jon S. Schmitt
Christopher J. Schouten
Tobias Schwarz
Jennifer Sebree
Mark S. Server
Scott B. Seymann
Raul Arthur H. Sibayan
Melvin O. Silao
Eric D. Simmons
Richard J. Simms
Leonard J. Simon
Colum Slevin
Kenneth V. Slevin
Maria A. Slevin
Jody M. Smaciarz
Jane M. Smethurst
R. Charles Smith
Stephen P. Smyth
Jeffrey A. Snodgrass
Sinead M. Somers
Robert J. Sprathoff
Gail L. Springsteen
Curt G. Spurging
Rebecca D. Stansbury
Elaine C. Blea Starace
Gabor T. Steisinger
Kenna D. Stevens
Renee L. Stigers
Annette M. Stone
James J. Stoyanof
Joanne I. Sugrue
Dana A. Sulceski
Helio Takahashi
Hugo M. Takahashi
Joseph M. Tangonan
Michael E. Tassoni
Danilo C. Taverna
Beverly J. Testa
Douglas B. Tinnin
Danilo I. Tolentino
Imelda B. Tolledo-Mondala
Fiona N. Trayler
Michael J. Tweedle
Howard D. Umfress
Jennifer C. Vallecorsa
Jamie M. Vallee
Kenneth D. Vallee
Wendo Van Essen
William E. Van Ness
Deborah D. Vercellino
Garilandy R. Vicuna
Vincente V. Villacorta
George P. Villaflor
Melanie S. Walchek
Declan B. Walsh
John R. Walsh
Mark K. Weathers
Clifton L. Wegener
Laura J. Wentworth
Thomas D. Wheeler
Suzanne L. Wilson
Wendy K. Wilson
James W. Wood
Fernando P. Xalabarder
Rolando F. Yago
Irina Yegorova
Salvador C. Young Jr.
Brandi J. Young
Diane M. Youngs
Rodrigo Q. Zafe Jr.
Emmanuel D. Zamora
Neil T. Zawicki
Evgenia Zimnukhova

Art Credits–Page 1: border design by Suzanne Lemieux Wilson; **2:** animation by John W. Hill; **2–3:** background by Robyn C. Nason; **5:** color key by Suzanne Lemieux Wilson; **11:** character art by Robyn C. Nason, border design by Suzanne Lemieux Wilson; **12:** art by Suzanne Lemieux Wilson; **13:** portrait by Suzanne Lemieux Wilson; **14–15:** color key by Kenneth V. Slevin; **16:** *(B)* color key by Kenneth V. Slevin; **16–17:** background by Richard A. Heichberger, **17:** *(B)* background by Winston B. Aquino; **18:** *(T)* background by Zoe J. Evamy, *(M)* background by Jocelyn D. Clemente, *(B)* color key by Mike Perezza; **18–19:** background by Phaedra Craig; **20:** layout by Sinead M. Somers; **21:** eagle layout by William C. Makra; **22–23.** conceptual art by Suzanne Lemieux Wilson; **24:** *(B)* background by Winston B. Aquino; **24–25:** background by Winston B. Aquino; **25:** *(B-L, B-R)* background by Micah R. Gosney; **26:** background by David M. Rabbitte; **27–28:** conceptual art by Suzanne Lemieux Wilson; **29:** layout designs by William C. Makra; **30:** *(T-L, T-R)* background by Winston B. Aquino; **30–31:** background by John C. Devlin; **33:** Romanov crest painted by Derek G. Holmes; **34:** Romanov portrait by Suzanne Lemieux Wilson; **35–38:** color key by Kenneth V. Slevin; **39–40:** background by Robyn C. Nason; **41:** Mike Perezza; **42:** *(B-L)* layout by Danilo I. Tolentino, *(B-R)* layout by Juan A. Luna; **42–43:** background by Paul M. Kelly; **43:** *(B)* layout by David J. Hardy; **44–45:** background by Robyn C. Nason; **46:** crest design by Suzanne Lemieux Wilson; **46–47:** background by Robyn C. Nason; **48–49:** background by Paul M. Kelly; **50–51:** background by John C. Devlin; **51:** *(T-L)* background by Zoe J. Evamy, *(T-R)* background by John C. Devlin; **52:** layout by Danilo I. Tolentino; **53:** layout by David J. Hardy; **54–55:** background by Robyn C. Nason; **55:** *(T)* background by Robyn C. Nason, *(M)* background by Kenneth V. Slevin, *(B)* background by Paul M. Kelly; **58:** conceptual design by Suzanne Lemieux Wilson; **60–61:** Pooka animation by Fernando Moro; **62:** *(B)* background by Joseph J. DeAsis; **62–63:** background by Henry D. McGrane; **63:** *(B)* background by Joseph J. DeAsis; **64:** *(T)* background by David M. Rabbitte, *(M, B)* Micah R. Gosney; **65:** portrait design by Suzanne Lemieux Wilson; **66:** *(T)* background by Robyn C. Nason; **66–67:** animation by John W. Hill, *(B)* background by Derek G. Holmes; **68–69:** layout designs by Sinead M. Somers, William C. Makra; **70:** *(T-L)* layout by George P. Villaflor, *(T-R)* layout by Philip A. Cruden, *(B)* layout by Stephen L. Holt; **71:** *(T)* layout by George P. Villaflor, *(M)* layout by Troylan B. Caro, *(B)* layout by Danilo C. Taverna; **72:** color keys by Richard C. Bentham; **73–80:** color keys by Kenneth V. Slevin; **81:** *(T)* background by Jocelyn D. Clemente, *(B)* background by Joseph M. Tangonan; **82–83:** *(T)* background by Richard A. Heichberger, *(B)* layout by William C. Makra; **84–85:** background by Richard A. Heichberger; **85:** *(T)* layout by Hung Yuan Chiang; **86–87:** background by Richard A. Heichberger; **87:** crest design by Suzanne Lemieux Wilson; **88–89:** background by Robyn C. Nason; **90:** *(T)* background by Robyn C. Nason, *(M)* background by Micah R. Gosney, *(B)* background by John C. Devlin; **90–91:** background by Zoe J. Evamy; **92–93:** background by Micah R. Gosney; **93:** *(T-L)* background by Derek G. Holmes, *(T-R)* background by David M. Rabbitte; **94–95:** animation by Leonard J. Simon; **96:** *(T)* background by David M. Rabbitte, *(M, B)* background by Winston B. Aquino; **97:** *(clockwise from T-R)* backgrounds by Robyn C. Nason, Winston B. Aquino, Paul M. Kelly, Winston B. Aquino, Winston B. Aquino, Micah R. Gosney, Micah R. Gosney; **98–99:** animation by John W. Hill; **100:** *(T)* layout by Danilo C. Taverna, *(M)* background by Micah R. Gosney, *(B)* layout by Martin G. Hanley; **101:** layout by Juan A. Luna; **102–105:** background by Robyn C. Nason; **106–107:** animation by Leonard J. Simon, color key by Kenneth V. Slevin; **107:** 3-D design by Thomas M. Miller; **108–109:** background by Henry D. McGrane; **109:** *(T)* background by Pio D. Ravago III, *(M)* background by Owen J. Rohu, *(B)* background by David W. Satchwell; **114:** background by Zoe J. Evamy; **115–118:** color key by Suzanne Lemieux Wilson; **119:** background by Zoe J. Evamy; **121:** color key by Richard C. Bentham; **122:** color key by Suzanne Lemieux Wilson; **123:** conceptual art by Suzanne Lemieux Wilson; **124:** color key by Suzanne Lemieux Wilson; **125:** color key by Suzanne Lemieux Wilson; **126:** *(T)* layout by Hung Yuan Chiang; **126–127:** *(B)* layout by Philip A. Cruden; **128–129:** color key by Suzanne Lemieux Wilson; **130–131:** layouts by Hung Yuan Chiang; **132–133:** layout by Hung Yuan Chiang; **134:** *(B-L)* layout by Stephen L. Holt, *(B-R)* layout by David J. Hardy; **134–135:** background by Xiao-Xia Cheng; **135:** *(B)* layout by Philip A. Cruden; **136:** *(B-L)* background by Zoe J. Evamy, *(B-R)* background by Pio D. Ravago III; **136–137:** background by Winston B. Aquino; **137:** *(B)* background by David M. Rabbitte; **138:** *(T-L, T-R)* layout by Danilo I. Tolentino; **138–139:** layout by Philip A. Cruden; **139:** *(T-L, T-R)* layout by Danilo I. Tolentino; **140–141:** layout by George P. Villaflor; **142:** *(T)* background by Pio D. Ravago III, *(M, B)* background by Xiao-Xia Cheng; **142–143:** background by Henry D. McGrane; **144–145:** color key by Kenneth V. Slevin; **146:** *(B)* background by Vic Villacorta; **146–147:** background by Jocelyn D. Clemente; **147:** *(B-L)* layout by Stephen L. Holt, *(B-R)* layout by Hung Yuan Chiang; **148:** *(B)* background by Micah R. Gosney; **148–149:** background by David M. Rabbitte; **149:** *(B-L)* background by Jocelyn D. Clemente, *(B-R)* background by David M. Rabbitte; **150–151:** backgrounds by Micah R. Gosney; **152–158:** backgrounds by Jocelyn D. Clemente; **159:** *(T)* layouts by Philip A. Cruden, *(B)* layout by Hung Yuan Chiang; **160:** layout by Philip A. Cruden; **161:** *(T)* background by Pio D. Ravago III, *(B)* color key by Richard C. Bentham; **162:** *(B)* background by Richard A. Heichberger; **162–163:** background by Jocelyn D. Clemente; **163:** *(B)* background by Robyn C. Nason; **164–165:** background by Micah R. Gosney; **170:** *(B)* background by Xiao-Xia Cheng; **170–171:** background by Zoe J. Evamy; **171:** *(B)* background by Phaedra Craig; **172–173:** background by Owen J. Rohu; **175:** background by Robyn C. Nason; **176–177:** color key by Richard C. Bentham; **177:** color key by Suzanne Lemieux Wilson; **178–179:** background by Paul M. Kelly; **180–181:** background by Joseph M. Tangonan; **182:** layout by Sinead M. Somers; **183:** *(L)* conceptual designs by James P. Bluth, *(R)* layouts by William C. Makra; **184:** *(T)* 3-D design by John P. Rand; **185:** background by Jocelyn D. Clemente; **186:** *(T)* background by Joseph M. Tangonan, *(M)* background by Pio D. Ravago III, *(B)* background by Phaedra Craig; **186–187:** background by Joseph M. Tangonan; **188–189:** background by Pio Ravago III; **189:** *(T)* Jocelyn D. Clemente, *(M)* Zoe J. Evamy, *(B)* Owen Rohu; **190–191:** Joy Clemente.